The Essentials of Commu

D0353127

Also by Peter Sharkey

Introducing Community Care

THE ESSENTIALS OF COMMUNITY CARE

A Guide for Practitioners

Peter Sharkey

Consultant Editor: Jo Campling

First published 2000 by
MACMILLAN PRESS LTD
Houndmills, Basingstoke, Hampshire RG21 6XS
and London
Companies and representatives
throughout the world

ISBN 0–333–77289–X

A catalogue record for this book is available
from the British Library.

This book is printed on paper suitable for recycling and
made from fully managed and sustained forest sources.

10 9   8   7   6   5   4   3   2   1
09 08 07 06 05 04 03 02 01 00

Printed in Great Britain

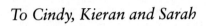

To Cindy, Kieran and Sarah

Contents

List of Figures

Introduction

This is a book for social care and health care practitioners (and those training in these disciplines). It is also a book for social policy students interested in community care and for anyone wanting an introductory overview of the main issues in community care.

Community care is a fascinating area of study, raising important questions about how we organise and care for the most vulnerable members of society, who should do that caring and who should pay for it. Underpinning discussions of community care are important questions of values, such as how much do we care for those adults in society who are most vulnerable and in what way should we care for them?

Community care is usually seen as being about social care and support for people in the community. However, health provision is a major dimension of any care within the community. Hence in this book the term 'practitioners' is often used as a generic term to describe community nurses, community occupational therapists, social workers and other professional workers involved in community care.

The book actively tries to put 'community' back into 'community care', based on the belief that this element has been neglected. My own practice involved both social work and community work and my teaching has encompassed community work and community care. There is much in common between these two areas and much that one side can learn from the other.

The present community care system, which developed during the early 1990s, was formulated when the government philosophy in relation to health and social care was one of expanding the role of the market. Those who supported this policy (and the wider expansion of the role of the market throughout society) were often called the 'New Right', and the changes in community care need to be understood within this wider context. New Right policies led to a curtailing of the powers of local authorities, a focus on the development of a competitive market, the development of a strong individualistic ethos and the targeting of individuals for provision and help. Within the book there will be some critique of this ideology. The emphasis on individual problems needs to be seen within the wider societal structures within which they are found. There are links to be made, for example, between poverty and mental health. Community care action and policy should be seen within the wider structural factors and the structural causes of poverty. We shall see that the policies of the 1980s and early 1990s individualised community care issues by emphasising individual packages of care and eligibility criteria. The targeting of particular people with severe problems has played a part in divorcing community care from the communities and societal structures within which it takes place. This book will try to make connections with the wider picture. This has been facilitated somewhat by the election of the Labour government in 1997, which at least acknowledged the links between, for example, health and inequality (DoH, 1999b) and developed policies to deal with social exclusion.

The current community care system is embedded in the National Health Service and Community Care Act 1990. Discussion of this Act is central to this book and the abbreviation NHS&CC Act 1990 is used throughout. The Act applied to all parts of the United Kingdom and therefore the community care systems of Scotland, Wales, Northern Ireland and England share many common features – some of the differences that do exist will be outlined in the text.

A book entitled *The Essentials of Community Care* involves some selection and some judgement about what the 'essentials' are. My judgements in this respect are based on over ten years of teaching and writing on the subject. The issues chosen are those of which a sound knowledge of the background context is vital if practitioners are to develop good, reflective practice. My personal belief is that community care developments have been too focused on providing individual solutions rather than addressing community issues. I also believe that they have failed adequately to address the relationship between practitioners and unpaid carers within the community. It is argued that new thought and attention needs to be given to these matters.

Chapter 1 outlines the background to the NHS&CC Act 1990, the changes it introduced to community care and the subsequent developments during the 1990s. The vast majority of community care is provided by relatives, neighbours and friends, and Chapter 2 focuses on this aspect of care in the community. A key question during the 1990s was 'who should provide what'. There have been particular tensions about and changes to the boundaries of health and social care provision. Chapter 3 outlines the background to this and the way in which the boundaries of community care provision have been shifting, using the long-term care of older people as an illustration. Probably the most significant change for practitioners after the passage of the NHS&CC Act 1990 was the introduction of care management, and this is the concern of Chapter 4. A variety of professional workers are involved in the delivery of community care provision and a central problem is the structures under which they have to work. These structures have often impeded their ability to work together, and this is the theme of Chapter 5, with particular reference to services for mental health service users. This links into the topic of the relationship between professional workers and informal care networks, which is central to the discussion in Chapter 6. Chapter 7 examines user empowerment, which has been part of the rhetoric about community care developments. How far the reality matches the rhetoric is examined. Child abuse has been a major concern of social and health care professionals for many years but the abuse of adults has not been given similar attention and concern. This is changing and I argue in Chapter 8 for the integration of community care policies with policies relating to the abuse of adults. Community care is not only about support (the theme of the earlier chapters), it can also involve and needs to involve some elements of control.

Some of the overarching themes of the book that cross different chapters and help to integrate the material are as follows:

- Working with and alongside the 'community' in relation to community care.
- Boundary problems between agencies.
- The importance of working constructively with other practitioners.
- Seeing 'individuals' within the wider structural context of their situation and the need for anti-oppressive practice to respond to this.
- The continuing tensions in health and social care between care and control.
- The importance of promoting independence and empowerment.

A summary of the subject matter to be covered is provided at the beginning of each chapter. In many chapters practice issues are threaded through the material, but all of the chapters end with a section on practice issues of concern and relevance to practitioners, followed by a list of further reading for those who wish to follow up a topic. Where helpful, a list of pertinent World Wide Web sites is also provided.

Terminology varies across professional groupings. In this book 'service user' is generally used to describe people who use community care services. Whilst perhaps not an ideal description, I hope it is an acceptable to the various professional groups and to service users themselves. In other areas of description an effort has been made to avoid terminology that might be seen as offensive or oppressive, and it is hoped that this aim has been achieved.

PETER SHARKEY

Several colleagues at Liverpool John Moores University have made comments on earlier drafts and I am grateful to them. Jo Campling has been a ready source of helpful advice. Thanks also to Macmillan's external reviewers for detailed and helpful comments.

■ *Chapter 1* ■

Background to Community Care

Chapter summary
This chapter covers: • The background to and community care content of the NHS&CC Act 1990. • Key aspects of what the government was trying to do in relation to social care and health care. • How local authorities responded to the financial pressures upon them. • The need to connect individual community care concerns to wider issues of public policy and structural inequality.

■ Introduction

Community care is hard to define. One broad understanding is the care of people within the community who have previously lived in long-stay institutions or asylums. A second element focuses on efforts to keep disabled people, older people and vulnerable people within the community rather than seeing them having to go into institutional care. A third key issue is the considerable unpaid support and help given by relatives, friends and neighbours.

In terms of those who receive care, it is possible to take a narrow definition of community care and see it as essentially the care within the community of older people, people with learning difficulties, people with physical disabilities and people with mental health problems. However a wider definition would include several other groups, for example:

• People with a sensory impairment.
• People with problems arising from the use of drugs or alcohol.
• Victims of domestic violence.
• Homeless people.
• Vulnerable single parents.
• People with HIV/AIDS.
• Ex-offenders.
• Refugees.
• People requiring palliative care.
• People now in the community after many years in hospital.

The great majority of community care is provided by informal carers, usually family members (this will be explored in detail in Chapter 2), which means that most of us have some personal experience of aspects of community care. These experiences can often open our eyes to the complexities and stresses of caring and issues concerning the services available. One personal experience is described in Box 1.

Box 1.1   *A personal experience*

In *Remind Me Who I Am Again* (1999), Linda Grant describes the life of her Jewish mother, especially during her later years, when she was disabled by dementia. In the book there are many insights into the disease, the dilemmas and emotions of caring, and the community care system. Grant was motivated to write the book 'Because there is a silence, a taboo. No one knows how to feel, or what to think because the meteor of dementia that strikes families and wipes out so much is supposed to be part of the realm of privacy. What you don't talk about. What you keep to yourself' (ibid., 1999, p. 300). Grant and others have begun to break the taboo of silence and provide us with powerful prose on the experiences and feelings involved. Many of us will experience something similar in our own personal lives.

Aspects of community care are quite commonly headlined in the media. Social workers may be blamed for 'bed-blocking' in hospitals through delays in assessment, an old person may die of abuse or neglect, or mental health services may be claimed to be in disarray following some incident. These are 'human interest' stories because they could relate so easily to ourselves, our family or our friends.

This chapter sets the scene for the later chapters by covering the changes in community care services during the 1990s, what the government was trying to achieve with the changes and how agencies responded. After the passage of the postwar welfare state legislation, with its background in the Beveridge Report, there were a number of white papers and reports on aspects of community care but little actual legislation. It is for this reason that the NHS&CC Act 1990 stands out as a major piece of legislation in the postwar period. Various postwar governments made some effort to develop community care policies, but these were not pursued with great energy or determination and by the mid 1980s most commentators and politicians of all political parties agreed that a lot was wrong with community care.

■ The social care changes

The Audit Commission's *Making a Reality of Community Care* (1986) was very critical of community care as it was operating. The report stressed the need for some urgent reform of the financing and organising of community care, 'The one option that is not tenable is to do nothing about present financial, organisational and staffing arrangements' (ibid., p. 4).

Central to its critique was the existence of 'perverse incentives' (DHSS funding) for care to be provided in residential and nursing homes but a lack of comparable funds to help those who preferred to remain in their own homes. It argued that 'Radical steps will be necessary if the underlying problems are to be solved. Fine-tuning the existing arrangements, or treating the symptoms, will not meet the needs of the situation' (ibid., p. 13).

The government responded to the Audit Commission's Report by commissioning a further report. The task was given to Roy Griffiths, who had already carried out work on the health services. According to Griffiths (1988):

- Better value could be obtained from the existing resources.
- At central government level community care was 'everybody's distant relative but nobody's baby' (ibid., p. iv). Hence there should be a minister in charge of community care.
- The existing organisational structures should remain in place but there was a need to spell out responsibilities and to insist on better performance and accountability.
- Packages of care arrangements for individuals should be made available, and there was also a need for care management.
- The lead authority in relation to community care should be the local authority.

Griffiths' recommendation about an increased role for the local authorities was not initially popular with the government. This was a government which had energetically tried to curb the power and influence of local authorities over the preceding years. The Griffiths Report was published in March 1988, but there was more than a year's delay before the government responded. A range of possible alternative ways of organising community care were apparently looked at before falling back on Griffiths' idea of local authority responsibility.

The Secretary of State for Health announced the government's main intentions to the House of Commons in July 1989. These were largely in line with Griffiths' recommendations but with a few differences, for example there was to be no single minister responsible for community care. This was followed by the publication of the White Paper *Caring for People* in November (DoH, 1989a). The White Paper contained two separate chapters on community care in Wales and Scotland – there was a separate White Paper for Northern Ireland (DHSS, 1990), reflecting the very different administrative arrangements there. Shortly after the publication of

Caring for People, the government introduced the National Health Service and Community Care Bill, which included provisions for implementing the plans set out in the White Paper. Between December 1989 and June 1990 the Bill progressed through parliament and received Royal Assent in late June 1990.

The community care aspects of the Act occupied only a few sections but they set the framework for community care provision over the following years. The Act was implemented in three stages between 1991 and 1993. The big change in relation to financing came in 1993 with the transfer of responsibilities and money to local social service authorities. After April 1993 prospective residents of residential and nursing homes had to approach these authorities rather than the Benefits Agency for help with fees.

Transferred money was paid through the Special Transitional Grant between 1993 and 1999. This was extra ring-fenced money that was paid on top of the money social service authorities received through the Standard Spending Assessment (the way in which most local authority finance from central government is allocated and distributed). The Conservative government insisted that 85 per cent of the transferred money be spent on independent providers rather than local authority providers. Ironically, in the absence of a significant independent domiciliary care market this requirement meant that most of the money for community care was initially spent on residential and nursing home care. The Labour government elected in 1997 removed the 85 per cent rule but brought in a new condition that involved the local authorities working closely with the NHS: part of the money had to be used to stop bed blocking and to develop home care services.

Some argue that community care law has remained in a poor shape since the 1990 Act, that it is deeply rooted in earlier legislation and leaves social service authorities and social workers open to litigation. Clements, for example, believes that the legislation needs to be unified and clarified and that 'Community care law is a hotchpotch of conflicting statutes, which have been enacted over a period of 50 years; each statute reflects the different philosophical attitudes of its time' (Clements, 1996, p. 10).

As the 1990s progressed some of the weaknesses of the 1990 community care legislation became clearer. For example it neglected carers and failed adequately to promote independent living by not allowing direct payments to be made to service users so that they could set up their own care management systems. Some of the faults were addressed by piecemeal legislation such as that on carers (Carers Recognition and Services Act 1995) and independent living (Community Care (Direct Payments) Act 1996).

In late 1998 a new White Paper for England was published, entitled *Modernising Social Services* (DoH, 1998a). White Papers with a largely similar content were published shortly afterwards for Northern Ireland, Scotland and Wales. These White Papers outlined the Labour government's future plans for social care. There were to be no dramatic changes, rather the emphasis would be on improving the existing facilities, or modernising rather than restructuring them. One of the most significant proposals was the setting up of Commissions for Care Standards. Local authorities would lose their inspectorial function and the new commissions would regulate residential and nursing homes and services run by the local authorities including domiciliary care. Another significant theme was the importance of organisations working together and breaking down the traditional divisions between health care and social care (this will be discussed further in Chapters 3 and 5).

Thus in relation to community care the Labour government broadly retained the objectives of the previous Conservative administration, so there was no dramatic change with the change of government. However Labour put greater emphasis on promoting people's independence, providing services more consistently across the country and making the system more centred on service users (DoH, 1998a). Several new initiatives were intended to contribute towards these objectives, including a national charter, an emphasis on prevention and rehabilitation, a National Carers' Strategy, National Service Frameworks for user groups, guidance on Fair Access to Care and Better Government for Older People (ibid.) Labour also appointed a Royal Commission on Long Term Care, which reported early in 1999 (RCLTC, 1999).

A range of people, groups and organisations are involved in community care, including family carers, neighbours, local organisations, housing authorities, voluntary organisations and private organisations. Coverage will be given to these later in the book, especially in Chapters 2 and 3. Special mention in this introductory chapter, however, needs to be given to the health services. Whilst local authorities have faced considerable changes in relation to community care, big changes have also taken place in the health services and many of these have affected community care. This is the next focus of our discussion.

■ Health care changes

Social care is only one element of the range of services that make up the jig-saw of community care. The NHS&CC Act 1990 shook up both the National Health Service and social service authorities in dramatic ways, mapping out a different and rather uncertain future for them and introducing new concepts to both: purchaser/provider, contracts, markets, consumerism and user-rights.

Most of the NHS&CC Act 1990 was actually concerned with changes to the health service. The background to these changes was contained in a government review of the health service and a White Paper, *Working for Patients* (DoH, 1989b). The government wanted an internal market to be introduced into the NHS, believing that this would encourage managers to be more efficient. In this internal market, each hospital or NHS community service unit would compete against others for contracts to care for a certain number of patients. In private industry such competition is supposed to keep prices low. The same principle was now applied to the health service and use of the term purchaser/provider split became commonplace.

Hospitals and NHS community services were encouraged to become independent trusts within the NHS, which gave them a good deal of freedom to organise their own affairs. Community nurses were increasingly employed by community trusts. Market ideas were also extended to GPs, who could opt to become budget-holding GPs, able to control their own budgets and negotiate with hospitals for the best deal for their patients. Practice nurses were increasingly employed in GP surgeries under these new fund-holding arrangements. In this way the 'new' NHS evolved through the creation of more trusts and GP fundholders.

During the early 1990s the NHS tried to differentiate its services into primary care and acute care. Once patients were no longer seen by the medical profession as in need of medical care, any subsequent care was seen as 'social care', organised and paid for by social service authorities or the individuals themselves, subject to means-testing. Long-stay hospital accommodation for older people continued to be phased out. The early 1990s saw the growth of considerable tension between social service authorities and health services over who was responsible for what (this will be looked at in more depth in Chapter 3). In 1995 some clarification was provided in a government circular (LAC(95)5), which stated that the NHS had responsibilities for continuing care in the areas of rehabilitation and recovery, palliative health care, respite care and community health service support.

The Labour government's approach to health was outlined in the White Paper, *The New NHS: Modern, Dependable* (DoH, 1997a). Similar proposals were put forward in separate White Papers for Scotland, Wales and Northern Ireland. There were three key elements of the government's health strategy with particular relevance for community care, as follows:

□ *The development of health improvement programmes (HImPs)*

HImPs are action programmes led by the health authority to improve health and health care locally. They involve NHS trusts, Primary Care Groups, and other primary care professionals working in partnership with the local authority and other local interests (DoH, 1997a). They are designed to cover the most important health needs of the local population, the main health care requirements of the local population, and the range, location and investment required in local health services. HImPs respond to the national priorities and targets set by the government and are intended to hold the structure together at the local level.

Each HImP incorporates Joint Investment Plans (JIPs) between health authorities and social service authorities, as first detailed in 'Better Services for Vulnerable People' (a Department of Health guided programme which targets partnership planning for vulnerable people rather than the entire community). The government has particularly stressed the need to improve the quality and availability of rehabilitation services. Community occupational therapy services are central to this.

☐ *Continuing emphasis on and development of primary care*

The terms primary, secondary and continuing care are sometimes used as a shorthand description of health service provision. Secondary care is broadly taken to mean hospital provision and historically the vast majority of NHS money has gone into hospital care. Continuing care is care that may be needed after hospital medical treatment and includes respite care, rehabilitative care and palliative care. Primary care is community-based care, and during the 1990s it was increasingly stressed that this should be given priority in terms of health service provision.

The Labour government elected in 1997 continued the emphasis on primary health care. Primary Care Groups would be set up (in Wales these were called Local Health Groups and in Scotland Local Healthcare Cooperatives), GP fund-holding as such would come to an end and the new Primary Care Groups would be led by GPs and community nurses and cover a population of about 100 000. GPs would thus have a central role in a further shift away from hospital and towards community care. Initially the Primary Care Groups would have an advisory role in relation to the local health authorities. At a later stage they would, as part of the health authority take devolved responsibility for the budget. In the third phase they would become free-standing bodies accountable to the health authority. Phase four would see them become Primary Care Trusts, commissioning all care and running community health services after merging with the existing community trusts. These GP groups or collectives could in time be responsible for spending a very considerable amount of NHS money on primary and secondary care. Social services personnel would be on the governing bodies of the Primary Care Groups.

These developments provide the potential for closer working relationships at the local level between practitioners such as GPs, community nurses, social workers and occupational therapists The government intends to expand the scope for closer cooperation between the health and social service authorities through, for example, the pooling of budgets.

☐ *An emphasis on preventive health*

The Labour government put particular emphasis on public health issues. It appointed a public health minister and the *Health of the Nation* strategy was replaced by a new strategy called *Our Healthier Nation*. The four countries of the UK each published a Green Paper on the way forward. These acknowledged the growing inequality between the health status of the rich and the poor, which the previous government had failed to do. This was a significant and important step forward. The new approach also stressed the importance of having a community work or community action element in its strategy. *Our Healthier Nation* set targets for improved public health in relation to cancer, strokes, accidents and mental health, to be achieved by 2010. Part of the strategy was also to devolve responsibility for tackling specific problems in the areas where they occurred. Three particular settings for action were identified as schools, workplaces and neighbourhoods. The English White Paper, *Saving Lives: Our Healthier Nation* (DoH, 1999b), added details to the proposals and set a target of saving 300 000 lives by 2010. It stressed the important role to be played by nurses and health visitors in health promotion.

Preventive measures have obvious implications for community care. The incapacitation of people through strokes and heart disease is a major factor in the demand for community care services, so the prevention of strokes, heart disease or accidents would reduce the pressure on community care resources. A lower incidence of cancer would reduce the need for palliative care. The human and social cost of mental distress is enormous and all attempts at prevention are important. Effective 'harm-reduction' policies in relation to drugs would result in fewer cases of HIV/AIDs and hepatitis B and C.

These preventive initiatives are important not only in themselves but also in experimenting with new relationships at the local level between workers and between professional workers and their communities. There are lessons to be learnt for wider community care from the work in preventive health.

Caring for People (DoH, 1989a) included a commitment to 'promote positive and healthy lifestyles among all age-groups through health education and the development of effective health surveillance and screening programmes' (ibid., p. 11), but the overall aim of the community care changes has been to target those in greatest need. In contrast the *Our Healthier Nation* strategy is about prevention. An overarching, inclusive framework that provides better links between community care and preventive health care measures needs to be developed. Simply targeting those in greatest need of community care could be seen as shortsighted. Better health and fitness in earlier years may well reduce the cost of long-term care in later life. Helping people with independent living, rehabilitation and convalescence needs to be part of the framework. Building a real 'community' dimension into community care work is an essential element of this, as well as a theme of this book, especially in Chapters 6 and 7.

■ Variations within the UK

There are some variations in community care provision in different parts of the UK. Wales and England have a shared legal system and community care developments in the two countries have been similar. The main difference is that Wales has had two all-Wales strategies: the All-Wales Mental Handicap (now Learning Difficulties) Strategy, launched in 1983, and the All-Wales Strategy on Mental Illness, launched in 1989. These have combined special earmarked money with Welsh Office guidance on the way in which services should be provided (Douglas and Philpot, 1998). Welsh local authorities also have to comply with the Welsh Language Act 1993, which gives members of the public the right to choose which language to use in their dealings with the authorities.

Northern Ireland has had a very different administrative structure as a result of direct rule in the province. With the introduction of direct rule an alternative had to be found to local government welfare provision. The pragmatic solution was to link this to the health service structure. This resulted in a unified health and social services structure under the auspices of four boards, set up in 1973 and accountable to Westminster through the Northern Ireland civil service and the Secretary of State. The board members were directly appointed by ministers. The boards have tended to be purchasers rather than providers and it has been trusts that have largely provided the services. If the 1998 Northern Ireland Agreement is implemented, local government will acquire executive and legislative powers and services such as health and social service trusts will be devolved to it.

The NHS&CC Act 1990 also applied to Scotland and so a similar system of provision and procedures has evolved there (Petch *et al.*, 1996). Some writers have noted that developments on the ground were perhaps slower in Scotland than elsewhere, and that the development of a mixed economy of care was also slower (Douglas and Philpott, 1998). There are some legal differences in some areas. For example, the Scottish law on property management on behalf of vulnerable adults is substantially different. The Social Services Departments of England and Wales are called Social Work Departments in Scotland. In this book the term 'social service authorities' will generally be used to cover both. The Scottish health boards are the equivalent of the health authorities of England and Wales.

The devolution changes have also introduced regional assemblies in England. While the local authorities have continued to be responsible for social services and social care since the devolution changes in Scotland, Wales and England, greater variation in community care provision may eventually emanate from the new Scottish Parliament and Welsh Assembly.

■ Key objectives of government policies

In relation to community care, the 1990 legislation contained a number of key policy objectives, some of which are summarised below.

□ *Control on expenditure*

In the 1970s supplementary benefits were administered in a way that gave considerable discretion to social security officers and local offices. One aspect of this was assisting residents of private residential or nursing homes who found themselves in financial difficulty. In 1979 only £10 million was spent in this way. From late 1980 the rules under which people could claim board and lodging expenses were regulated by parliamentary statute and residents or boarders could claim full board and lodging plus an amount to cover personal expenses. Local authorities under financial pressure need no longer build new residential homes, and health authorities could close long-stay wards without appearing heartless. As Lewis and Glennerster (1996, p. 4) wrote, 'In short, the social security budget had come to the rescue of families, local authorities, and the NHS, all of them under tight budgetary limits and increasing demand'.

During the 1980s there was a rapid rise in social security payments to people in residential and nursing homes – from £10 million in 1979 to £2600 million in 1993 (Richards, 1996, p. 9). Concern about the exponential growth of this expenditure was reflected in various reports and in *Caring for People* (DoH, 1989a). No one was required to assess whether a person really needed residential or nursing home care. This issue was a cause of concern to the Audit Commission and featured in the Griffiths Report, and according to Lewis and Glennerster (1996, p. 8) it is crucial to understanding the subsequent reforms: 'They were driven by the need to stop the haemorrhage in the social security budget and to do so in a way which would minimise political outcry and not give additional resources to the local authorities themselves'. Lewis and Glennerster argue that: 'What was new in the 1980s was the runaway cost of giving families what amounted to an open cheque book to buy residential and nursing home care – the most expensive kinds of alternatives available. No government could have let such a situation continue' (ibid., p. 195). Their view is that the government's prime objective was to check public spending and if possible reduce it.

□ *The development of social care markets*

A second policy goal of the Conservative government was to develop a market in social care. How this might be done was left largely to the local social service authorities, but they were expected to establish a purchaser/provider split. The 85 per cent rule (whereby 85 per cent of the

Special Transitional Grant money had to be directed towards independent providers) had a considerable impact on the development of independent social care provision (Wistow *et al.*, 1996; Lewis and Glennerster, 1996) and the social care market. Lewis and Glennerster go so far as to write that 'The most significant central government intervention in the field of community care was the imposition of the 85 per cent rule late in 1992' (ibid., p. 200). A further boost to the social care market was provided by a Department of Health directive (LAC(92)27) which gave individual users the right to enter the home of their choice, within certain financial limits. A later directive (LAC(93)4) required the social service authorities to consult the independent sector when preparing community care plans. There thus developed a market in social care, accompanied by growing acceptance of the idea (Wistow *et al.*, 1996). Different organisational structures evolved but all adapted to the purchaser/provider split, the increased amount of independent provision and the regulation of this provision through contracts.

The development of social care markets complemented the development of internal markets within the NHS. Also, in its effort to contain costs the government tried to shift some of the 'free' health care costs across to the means-tested social care sector. Continuing care provision was run down within the NHS during the early 1990s, often leaving social service authorities with increased problems and expenditure. This 'cost-shunting' is covered in Chapter 3.

☐ *Achieving a seamless service*

Throughout the postwar period problems arose in respect of different agencies working together well and effectively, and joint working from the mid 1970s only led to some marginal improvements in some areas. The problem was often exacerbated by the existence of different geographical boundaries for the health care and social care authorities.

The 1990 DoH Policy Guidance document referred to the aim of 'seamless care', suggesting that users should not be conscious of organisational divisions in the delivery of services. Adding to the previous problems were the problems thrown up by the purchaser/provider split within social service authorities. Perhaps more typical than a 'seamless service' was a pattern of buck-passing and cost-shunting between agencies, with consequent frustrations for service users. Government policy since 1997 has put even more emphasis on achieving a seamless service and to this end a number of incentives have been introduced, as well as some legislative changes. Chapter 5 deals with this in detail.

☐ *Quality assurance*

A fourth policy objective was to set up a system of quality assurance. By

April 1991 each social service authority had to have a complaints procedure and an inspection unit to inspect all homes for adults. This was the first step towards ensuring that all authorities had some basic mechanisms for checking on quality and rectifying problems. A further move was made in 1996, when local authorities were required to produce Community Care Charters, which set out the standards by which services would be delivered and monitored. Under the Labour government the emphasis has been on 'best value', which applies to all local government services and involves continuous improvement against a range of criteria.

☐ Increased choice

The above mentioned 'choice directive' (LAC(92)27) obliged authorities to respect the client's choice of residential or nursing home. The objective of all the changes was, according to the minister responsible, to improve the outcome for both users and carers, especially in terms of enhancing 'choice and independence' (DoH, 1989a, p. 4). The ministerial foreword to *Caring for People* clearly stated that its purpose was to 'give people a much better opportunity to secure the services they need and will stimulate public agencies to tailor services to individual's needs. This offers the prospect of a better deal for people who need care and for those who provide care. Our aim is to promote choice as well as independence' (ibid.)

☐ Care management

Finally, care management was introduced as a policy objective. This involved arranging a package of community services that would enable people to remain at home rather than go into residential care. Care management was a new way of working and was intended to provide an effective service to those in greatest need. It had been suggested in the Griffiths Report and was seen as an important part of the changes in *Caring for People* (DoH, 1989a). The form taken by assessment and care management was secondary to the government's main purpose and this partly explains why there has been considerable variation in the way in which it has developed. Chapter 4 looks at care management in detail.

■ How did local authorities respond to the funding pressures?

It was argued above that curbing social security spending was at the heart of the government's policy. The community care measures imposed on the local authorities were used as a way of limiting or capping the increasing social security spending. However, within a matter of months many local authorities were finding it hard to meet the financial demands of community care. They responded to the funding problem in a number of ways, including lobbying the government, expecting more from the voluntary sector and ensuring that services users were receiving their full benefit entitlement. The main mechanisms they used to stay within their budgets are outlined below.

☐ *The tightening of eligibility criteria*

Local authorities were asked to set up eligibility criteria so that staff and users could be clear about who was entitled to a service. A typical set of criteria is shown in Box 1.2:

Box 1.2   *An example of eligibility criteria*

- Category 1, high priority: an emergency or crisis point has been reached.
- Category 2, medium priority: a high level of need is assessed.
- Category 3, low priority: a need appears to exist and a response from the social service authority is appropriate.
- Category 4, non-priority: help may be desirable but it is not essential that it comes from the social service authority.

One way of coping with budgetary pressure was to tighten the way the eligibility criteria were operated. For example in year 1 (1993–94) an authority may have had sufficient resources to respond to categories 1, 2 and 3. However in later years it may have only been able to respond to categories 1 and 2. If financial pressures continued to mount it would have to look again at the criteria – one strategy is obviously to restrict its response to situations in category 1. At the end of 1994 Gloucestershire County Council announced that it could provide emergency care only to people who were 'at immediate physical risk' – presumably category 1 of their eligibility criteria.

The Audit Commission has urged local authorities to set eligibility criteria to fit their budget allocations. Eligibility criteria 'should be set at such a level that authorities can meet the needs of those who qualify and still keep within budget' (Audit Commission, 1996, p. 10). It is through the eligibility criteria that resources are rationed, that is, 'need' is equated with 'resources available'. This mechanism severely limits the idea that provision can be determined either by need or by the right to services.

Authorities have also made use of decision-making panels – by channelling all requests through such panels a tight check can be maintained on resources. Many practitioners now spend a lot of time 'managing rationing' rather than providing direct care.

The Labour government acknowledged this problem in *Modernising Social Services*: 'Eligibility criteria are getting ever tighter and are excluding more and more people who would benefit from help but who do not come into the most dependent categories' (DoH, 1998a, para. 2.3). This raised the question of whether there could be an alternative to the situation of tighter and tighter eligibility criteria providing services to the few (the targeted).

☐ *Cut Current Services*

Some authorities have responded to their funding problems by cutting services. A key aim of the reforms was to focus provision on those defined as in the greatest need. This has necessarily meant that people with less acute needs have had their services cut. For example up to 1500 people were affected in September 1994 when Gloucestershire Social Services cut its community care services to reduce its overspend. The necessity of Gloucestershire cutting its social services budget by £2.5 million and its inability to raise extra resources were due to rate capping procedures. The issue at stake was whether local councils should take their resources into account or whether they had a 'duty to care'. This tension between needs and resources is well-illustrated by the Gloucestershire judgement, described in Box 1.3.

Box 1.3   *The Gloucestershire judgement*

One of the 1500 affected by the social service cuts in Gloucestershire in 1994 was 78 year-old Michael Barry, who lived alone at home, could walk only with a zimmer frame due to a fractured hip, had suffered a stroke, several heart attacks and some sight loss, and had no contact with his family. Gloucester Social Services withdrew all help with cleaning and laundry, although they continued to provide help with shopping and meals on wheels

Michael Barry and a number of others applied for judicial review of the decision. The case went to the High Court, the Appeal Court and eventually the House of Lords. In March 1997 the Law Lords ruled by a majority of three to two that Gloucestershire County Council was within the law in withdrawing home help services from this elderly disabled man. The majority of judges backed the council's argument that resources, as well as need, should be taken into account when deciding on the provision of services.

Lord Nicholls wrote of the need to 'recognise that needs for services cannot sensibly be assessed without having some regard to the cost of providing them. A person's need for a particular type or level of services cannot be decided in a vacuum from which all considerations of cost have been expelled' (transcript of judgement).

The dissenting voices were those of Lord Lloyd and Lord Steyn. Lord Lloyd said that Gloucestershire had been placed in an 'impossible position' by government spending cuts. 'The solution lies with the Government. The passing of the Chronically Sick and Disabled Persons Act 1970 was a noble aspiration. Having willed the end, Parliament must provide the means' (transcript of judgement).

□ *Limiting the cost of care packages*

Most authorities put a limit on the care packages they are prepared to fund, although there is variation between authorities. Once it becomes more expensive for the authority to fund someone living in the community than it would be to contribute to their residential or nursing care, then this indicates the top end of any package that is likely to be funded for an extended period. Someone in a residential or nursing home receives a small allowance for personal expenditure and pays towards the cost of living there through his or her pension, income support or residential allowance. Thus the net cost to a local authority of providing a place in an average-cost residential home after the resident's own payments are taken into account may be somewhere in the region of £100 rather than the £250 or so charged by the home. This is the figure that many authorities set as the maximum they will pay for a package of care within the community. If they are very short of money they may reduce this limit. *Modernising Social Services* acknowledged the problem: 'The evidence is that many authorities are setting a financial ceiling on their domiciliary care packages, particularly in services for older people, which can lead to premature admissions to care homes when care at home would have been more suitable' (DoH, 1998a, para. 2.7).

Where care packages involve placement in a residential or nursing home, then a further way of responding to funding pressures has been to cut the amount paid to the independent providers of this care. One consequence of this is that the latter may feel forced to cut back on activities and other provisions for residents.

□ *Reviewing charging policy*

Section 17 of the Health and Social Services and Social Security Adjudication Act 1983 gave local authorities the power to recover 'such charge (if any) as they consider reasonable'. The power to charge is discretionary but the government assumed that local authorities would recover 9 per cent of their gross expenditure on non-residential community care through charges. In a survey the charity Mencap found that 95 per cent of local authorities in England and Wales were charging for non-residential community care services (Mencap, 1999). Charges were introduced or increased for a range of service provisions during the 1990s as a means of raising further money. Mencap argued that many families were in the Catch-22 position of not being able to cope without services but being unable to afford them. Charging policies and charging levels varied considerably between authorities. *Modernising Social Services* deemed this as unacceptable (DoH, 1998a, para. 2.29) and steps were to be taken to establish greater equity between local authorities.

□ *Personal savings*

Regulations stipulated that local authorities must partly subsidise a residential placement for someone with savings of between £10 000 and £16 000. Below £10 000 the council has to meet the full cost, apart from a small contribution from the resident's income support. However Sefton Council refused to pay the home care fees of nearly 50 elderly people, requiring them to spend all but £1500 of their own capital on fees. Help the Aged and the Public Law Project took the council to court and some aspects of Sefton's position were upheld by the High Court in a judicial review in early 1997. The case then went to the Appeal Court, where Sefton lost, as outlined in Box 1.4.

Box 1.4   The Sefton judgement

Mrs Blanchard moved from hospital to a nursing home. As her savings amounted to a little over £16 000 her family made the necessary arrangements with the nursing home. When her savings fell below £16 000 she applied for an assessment but Sefton Council refused to accept responsibility for her care. She challenged the decision in the High Court. The council argued that it should not have to pay for care if the residents had enough money to pay for it themselves. The High Court judged in favour of the council but this judgement was overturned by the Appeal Court and Mrs Blanchard won.

In spite of the Sefton judgement the charity Help the Aged claimed in 1998 that it had evidence that a number of local authorities were continuing to force elderly people to use their savings to pay nursing and residential home fees (*Community Care*, 23–29 July 1998, p. 1). The government clarified the situation through the Community Care (Residential Accommodation) Act 1998, which stipulated that once an older person's assets fell below £16 000 the local authority had a legal duty to contribute towards the cost of his or her care. The Act stated that there should be no 'undue delay' between the time when a person's assets fell below £16 000 and the time when the authority started to pay. There remained a concern that authorities might delay taking action and that as a consequence people's savings would continue to decline.

■ The wider context

When discussing community care it is possible to keep a narrow focus on legislative requirements and practitioner issues to do with care management and coping with limited resources. Community care can be interpreted as being limited to targeting those in greatest need of care packages. The changes within social service authorities (usually a split between child care and adult care), the emphasis on the market economy and the purchaser/provider split, and the focus on individuals has meant that the provision of community care has been reduced to individual assessments of packages and has lost touch with the wider processes. There is a need to see community care in the wider context of societal and social policy influences. Related issues include poverty, racism, ageism, domestic and sexual violence, homelessness, unemployment, poor housing and the activities of or power wielded by drug dealers and the alcohol and brewing industry.

Traditionally, health care has been very much located in individual diagnosis and treatment, although public health approaches have usually taken a much wider perspective. In the nineteenth century charitable welfare organisations were concerned with identifying and helping the 'deserving' poor, and at present there seem to be parallels between this and the community care guidance on 'targeting those in greatest need'. Just as in the nineteenth century there were those who argued against the philosophy of individualistic help to the deserving poor, there is a need in the present era to reject a definition of community care that is solely about those in greatest need. Now as then there are wider issues that need to be addressed.

Social care and health care always takes place in this broader political context. With the individualising process inherent in the community care changes it has sometimes been easy to lose sight of this. C. Wright Mills argued more than forty years ago that the sociological imagination was important in making connections between 'personal troubles' and 'the public issues of social structure' (Mills, 1959). The need for the sociological imagination to make these links is as important in the new millennium as it was for Mills in the 1950s. Practitioners need to understand these 'public' issues and try to incorporate this understanding into their practice, difficult though this can sometimes be. These issues include the growth of poverty, race discrimination, the exclusion of mental health service users, discrimination against and homophobia towards gay and lesbian people, the exclusion and stigmatisation of people with learning difficulties, and discrimination against older people. There is a desire among many practitioners to design a practice method that addresses these issues rather than ignores them.

Race discrimination, for example, was not addressed in the Audit Commission's report of 1986 and was only briefly addressed in the Griffiths Report (1988) and the White Paper (DoH, 1989a). The NHS&CC Act 1990 was silent on race, despite there being many issues of concern (Ahmad and Atkin, 1996). It has taken pressure and a number of initiatives to make progress on this. A report on eight authorities by the Social Services Inspectorate in 1998 entitled, *They Look After Their Own, Don't They?* (DoH, 1998b) indicated that although some progress had been made, black and ethnic minority older people were subject to significant disadvantage in gaining access to community care services. Most community care plans and charters failed to include specific statements about black elderly people and did not detail action plans to combat discrimination.

Similarly practitioners need to have the imagination to confront the homophobia faced by gay or lesbian service users within the context of a society that discriminates against them and has made few attempts to ensure that services and organisations are sensitive to their needs (Brown, 1998).

The community care changes of the early 1990s gave attention to some neglected groups of people and this was welcome. Community care users and provision needed to come more into the mainstream. In the late 1990s the Labour government put the tackling of 'social exclusion' at the centre of its programme. Many community care service users experience social exclusion and this emphasis provided the opportunity to bring both services and users more into the mainstream.

'Social exclusion' is now a commonly used term to describe social division in European societies. It has been used a good deal in relation to the social policy of the European Union. In this broad area social work can play a part through ideas/practice on empowerment and community work. Community work and community social work have had a long tradition within and alongside social work, and have much to offer to tackle exclusion and bring about social inclusion.

There is renewed interest in the regeneration of the poorest areas, which often have a high proportion of community care concerns. For example there are high concentrations of people with mental health problems or drug/alcohol problems in poor areas of cities. Problems that afflict whole communities are not best addressed by individualistic actions by reactive services (Barr *et al* 1997). Whilst there has been a history of regeneration policies going back thirty years, during the 1980s and early 1990s the emphasis was on economic objectives and the role of the private sector, with the aim of increasing inward investment into certain areas in need of regeneration. More recent policies and approaches have included a social dimension. Health Action Zones, alongside other initiatives such as the Single Regeneration Budget, Education Action Zones and Employment Action Zones are part of a set of policies to tackle social exclusion. Government policy documents now repeatedly stress the strong association between ill-health and low income (DoH, 1999b). The attention given by the government to poverty, exclusion and poor neighbourhoods has opened up opportunities for community care practitioners to relate their practice to these wider issues. These developments represent a welcome recognition of the 'structural' issues that affect community care. Social care and health care practitioners can play an important part in this process.

■ Practice issues

This chapter has outlined the very considerable changes in the health and social care services, and practitioners have had to find a new role for themselves within the remit of these changes. In spite of some of the frustrations caused by the changes, they have focused welcome attention on groups that have been traditionally neglected.

The changes have also raised some fundamental questions about the role of practitioners. For example many social workers have complained about mountains of paperwork, their inability to practice social work skills and the frustration of working within the eligibility criteria. It has been difficult to find a path through the paperwork, increased bureaucracy and personal stress. Some of the more innovative social work has taken place in the voluntary sector.

Community nursing and workloads also changed dramatically during the 1990s (Audit Commission, 1999). Community nurses are managing complicated treatments in the community that previously took place in hospitals, and they are nursing far more terminally ill people at home. Most of the bathing and putting-to-bed provision is now done by home care services (ibid.)

This chapter has suggested that there are links to be made by practitioners between personal troubles and public issues (Mills, 1959), hard though it can be to raise one's focus above the pressing individual needs that present themselves. This links into the possibilities of anti-oppressive practice and the debates on it. These themes will be returned to later in the book.

Since the election in 1997 of the Labour government, health and social care agencies have had to adapt to a large number of changes and initiatives. As the new government's policies took shape, certain themes emerged, such as interagency working, preventive health, the tackling of exclusion and user involvement. These topics are covered in Chapters 5 and 7. Links should be made by practitioners between the users of community care services and some of these policies, especially with regard to social exclusion, regeneration and preventive health.

What is needed is imaginative practice that works with and alongside the community and uses limited resources (such as practitioners' time and energy) to good effect. It is hoped that this book will play a small part in providing ideas and encouragement.

□ *Further reading*

W. I. U. Ahmad and K. Atkin (eds), *Race And Community Care* (Buckingham: Open University Press, 1996): a good critical introduction to the subject of race and community care.

B. Dimond, *Legal Aspects of Care in the Community* (London: Macmillan, 1997).

This book is particularly concerned with the health aspects of community care and tries to make the law understandable to the practitioner.

D. Hennessy (ed.) *Community Health Care Development* (London: Macmillan, 1997). This is an edited collection on the impact of the changes of the 1990s on community nurses and the people with whom they work.

R. Means and R. Smith *Community Care: Policy And Practice*, 2nd edn (London: Macmillan, 1998): a useful overview and background study of community care.

☐ *World Wide Web sites*

The Department of Health site provides a lot of information. In particular, circulars and the full text of recent Green Papers and White Papers can be studied at

http://www.open.gov.uk/doh/dhhome.htm

Policy changes in Scotland can be found at

http://www.scotland.gov.uk

in Wales at

http://www.cymru.gov.uk

and in Northern Ireland at

http://www.nio.gov.uk

The Health Education Authority has a good and popular site for issues connected with preventive health at

http://www.hea.org.uk/

■ *Chapter 2* ■

Care within the Community

Chapter summary
This chapter covers:
• The interweaving of formal and informal care.
• The different ways in which service agencies respond to carers.
• Data on carers from surveys and research studies.
• An analysis of why people care and an exploration of the complexity of caring.
• The tension between a focus on carers and a focus on independent living.
• Carers and assessment.

■ Introduction

It was stressed in Chapter 1 that the vast majority of community care has been and is provided by informal carers. This chapter focuses on the role of carers. The provision of care within the community is a fascinating topic and all readers will have some information and insights from their own lives upon which to draw. Many will be involved in caring and can reflect on why it is done, how much is done, their feelings about it and their feelings about others doing less or more. Even those without direct experience may have relatives or friends who can provide guidance. *Community Care in the Next Decade and Beyond* (DoH, 1990) provided some guidance on taking the preferences of carers into account and indicated that in some circumstances there might be a need for a separate assessment. Pressure for better legislation resulted in The Carers (Recognition and Services) Act 1995, which was implemented in April 1996. The Carers Act was primarily concerned with informal carers who provided or intended to provide regular and substantial care. It was left to local authorities themselves to define 'regular' and 'substantial' and to publicise that locally, although 20 hours per week was often taken as an indication of substantial care (Heron, 1998). Importantly, the Act recognised the contribution and particular circumstances of young carers. In 1999 the Labour government published a national strategy for carers called *Caring About Carers* (DoH, 1999a), which acknowledged the contribution made by carers and outlined ways in which more support and help could be given to them.

Carers are now organised into an effective support and lobbying organisation and this was important in bringing about the 1995 legislation as well as the national strategy. The Carers National Association was formed in 1988 and in addition to its 120 branches there are more than 220 carers' groups (CNA, 1998). This is a good example (of which there are many in community care) of collective issues of concern being addressed by small local organisations or a national voluntary organisation. The individual concerns of carers can be shared with others and channelled at the national level. Practitioners need to see beyond the individual and pay attention to these wider collectivities perhaps by assisting the development of a group or helping a carer to join a group. Working with groups and collectivities in this way not only utilises the skills of community workers but also allows practitioners to make links between personal troubles and public issues (as advocated at the end of Chapter 1).

Hadley and Clough (1996, p. 207) argue that at the core of the Thatcherite project was the notion of 'the self-interested individual pursuing his or her own maximum good'. There are alternatives to this view, one being the idea of 'mutuality', as outlined by Holman (1993). Indeed it can be argued that the very basis of community care is such mutuality. Most care in the community is provided by informal carers, especially partners and adult children. Among the many reasons why people become involved are love, duty and obligation – the basic ingredients of mutuality. A sensible system of community care needs to be based on this mutuality – to work with it and foster it. In reality, however, the community care system is based on another set of values and beliefs that revolve around the primacy of market ideas espoused by the New Right.

In the early 1980s government publications moved from talking about care *in* the community to care *by* the community:

> Whatever level of public expenditure proves practicable and however it is distributed, the primary sources of support and care for elderly people are informal and voluntary. These spring from personal ties of kinship, friendship and neighbourhood. They are irreplaceable. It is the role of public authorities to sustain and where necessary develop – but never to displace – such support and care. Care in the community must increasingly mean care by the community (DHSS, 1981, p. 3).

This is often quoted in books on community care because of the stress on '*by* the community'. Certainly, social scientists would emphasise how much care has always been undertaken by the community. Communities vary and the care provided within them varies according to the nature and history of each locality. Key questions for social scientists and practitioners working in neighbourhoods are:

- Who is doing the caring?
- Is it friends, neighbours or relatives (informal care)?

- What proportion of care is given by state services (formal care)?
- Has the amount of care provided by these two sectors changed?
- In what ways will the changing demographic patterns affect the patterns of care in the future?

In this complex area it is important for practitioners to have a vision because there has to be an interlinking of formal and informal care – ideally a balanced partnership without one exploiting the other. This can perhaps be obtained through the notion of 'interweaving' (Bulmer, 1987), where the formal services and the informal sector cooperate in a spirit of partnership and mutual trust, as described by Bayley in the early 1970s:

> The social services seek to interweave their help so as to use and strengthen the help already given, make good the limitations and meet the needs. It is not a question of the social services plugging the gaps but rather of their working with society to enable society to close the gaps (Bayley, 1973, p. 343).

■ The response of service agencies to carers

The relationship between service provision and carers is uncertain and ill-defined. Twigg and Atkin (1994) draw on Twigg's (1989) earlier work and propose four models:

- *Carers as resources.* In this model agencies regard carers as a type of resource. Agencies focus mainly on dependent people or the cared for and informal carers are only a background to these. They are a vital resource but not the primary subject of the agency's concern. Thus concern for carer welfare in this model is very limited.
- *Carers as co-workers.* In this model agencies see themselves as working alongside and in parallel with carers. The main image here is one of 'interweaving', which was referred to above as an appropriate aim for practitioners. The model encompasses the carer's interests and well-being.
- *Carers as co-clients.* Here the carer is seen as a client, as someone in need of help in his or her own right. This model tends to be applied to cases where a lot of care is needed and the carer is very stressed. The aim of intervention is to relieve carer strain, and the conflicts of interest between carer and dependant are fully recognised.
- *The superceded carer.* With the superceded carer the aim is not to support the care-giving relationship but to transcend or supercede it. There are two routes to this. One route starts with the disabled person and a desire to maximise his or her independence. The more this is achieved the more the carer and the disabled person are freed from the caring

relationship. The other route starts with concern for the carer and freeing him of her from the caring role.

In their overview of how health and social services staff respond to family carers, Twigg and Atkin (1994) suggest that there may be a tendency for medical staff to regard carers as a resource whereas social care professionals tend to be more aware of carers as co-clients. Consider the above models in relation to the case study in Box 2.1. What are the key issues in this case study? Do the models help to clarify the issues or suggest different approaches?

Box 2.1   Case study

Jim, an autistic young man in his twenties, has been looked after at home by his parents all his life. His parents have done most things for him. He is not able to cook for himself or shop and has very few relationships. Most of his time is spent watching television. Since leaving school there have been attempts to persuade him to attend a day centre but he usually refuses to go. Jim now says that he wants to leave home. His parents fear that he will not cope and will become isolated and depressed without their ongoing support.

Jim's scenario is very briefly sketched out and therefore only initial ideas can be drawn out. With the first model (carers as resources) the practitioner would focus on Jim, with the parents in the background as a resource depending on what was identified as being needed by and for him. In the second model (carers as co-workers) an alliance is likely between the carers and the practitioner, with Jim's expressed wishes being a little less to the fore than in model 1. With the third model (carers as co-clients) equal attention will be given to Jim and his parents. Assuming he wants help to live independently, then help will also be given to the parents in terms of helping them to adjust to the idea and its actuality. The fourth model (the superceded carer) seems rather similar but the idea is that eventually the care-giving relationship will become redundant. Jim will receive a lot of help to live independently, and a lot of support, counselling and assistance will be given to his parents to help them see their role differently.

The models can aid analysis. Change may of course be very difficult as Jim and his parents may have quite set patterns of behaviour and views. Nolan *et al.* (1996) query whether any of the models are appropriate. They suggest that a clearer partnership is required and that 'carers as experts' would be a more appropriate model. 'Here the explicit purpose is to increase carers' competency, to move them as rapidly as possible from "novice" to "expert" and to sustain them in the expert role throughout the various stages of the caregiving trajectory' (ibid., p. 156).

■ Factors that affect caring

All caring situations are influenced by the nature of social policies and practices as well as family and personal factors. This will be illustrated in this section by discussing demographic changes, changes in employment patterns and changes in marriage/living patterns.

The composition of the UK population in terms of age is changing quite dramatically. The two main reasons for this are the fall in the birth rate and the fact that people are living longer. It is expected that in 2001 the proportion of elderly (65+) people in the population will be six times greater than in 1901, while the number of those aged 85 and over will have increased 25-fold (Grundy, 1995, p. 1). Projections suggest that by 2026 those aged 65 and over will be twice that of 1961 and that the size in population aged 85 and over will have increased by more than five-fold (ibid., p. 2).

These figures suggest that the rise in demand for family care and health/social services provision could be substantial. The current figures and future projections suggest that the care of older people must be a major concern for community care as an increasing number of people will reach a point above the age of 80 where they cannot fully care for themselves. Whilst the fact that more people are living longer is to be welcomed, the figures do have implications for community care and for health and social services provision. It is not clear how informal and formal systems of care will respond to these demographic pressures. There will be an increasing need for services for older people and for additional resources to fund them. In comparison with earlier generations, people nowadays have fewer children and grandchildren, hence the care of older people will be provided by a much smaller number of young people than in the past.

A second factor affecting caring is the significant change in employment patterns. There has been a considerable increase in the number of married women participating in the labour market, making them less available for care provision. At the time of the 1931 census 10 per cent of married women were employed. In 1951 the figure had risen to 30 per cent, reaching 60 per cent by 1987. Almost all this increase was accounted for by part-time employment (Kiernan and Wicks, 1990, p. 26).

Kiernan and Wicks note that each successive group of new mothers returns to the labour market more quickly than the one before, and in recent years women's employment patterns have become more like those of men. Nonetheless, many mothers with dependent children are still likely to be working part-time, either through choice or because of a lack of adequate child care provision. These trends have led to a rise in the number of 'dual worker' families, that is, both parents go out to work: over half (52 per cent) of families with children consist of married couples who are both working (ibid., pp. 26–7). It does seem likely that these employment factors will limit the number of adult daughters and sons who are prepared to take on significant caring roles (Finch, 1995, p. 61).

A further factor in employment patterns is job mobility. Many people have to move in order to find a job, necessitating a choice between finding paid work or taking care of a dependent relative. These decisions are and will continue to be affected by how satisfactory caring alternatives are perceived to be.

A third factor affecting caring is the change in patterns of living. Data on this usually comes from national surveys, which are often not sensitive to changes within black and ethnic minority communities, and there is little data in rerspect of lesbian and gay people. Some key points provided by the Family Policy Studies Centre (1997) are shown in Box 2.2.

Box 2.2   Changes in patterns of living

- Just under one in ten adults are in a cohabiting relationship, rising to one in five among younger age groups.
- Two in five new marriages are likely to end in divorce.
- Seven in ten divorcing couples have children.
- Over a third of births are outside marriage.
- One fifth of families with children are headed by a lone parent.

The key question in terms of community care is how these changes in living patterns will affect community care. Some issues here are:

- Given the increase in the divorce rate, cohabitation and lone-parent families, what are the implications of this change when so much informal care is provided by spouses?
- Given the increase in births outside marriage, divorce and the number of step-children, what are the implications in terms of care by children? Will children provide as much informal care as in the past?
- With the changes in employment patterns and more women working, will women provide as much care as they have in the past?
- With the demographically ageing population, will old people care or be able to care for very old people?
- With changing attitudes towards care, duty and obligation, to what extent will adults want to impose on or trouble their children?

The statistics in Box 2.2 indicate that family life in Britain is undergoing unprecedented change (see also Clarke, 1995). Family care has been and still is the mainstay of community care. Although dramatic changes have occurred within the family it is not necessarily the case that feelings of kinship and obligation will decline (Finch, 1995). However it does seem likely that the pool of carers will decline and that there may be an impact on people's sense of duty and obligation, leading to less family care.

■ Who are the carers?

There was a considerable growth of interest in and research on informal caring during the 1980s and 1990s, providing us with some understanding of the origins, incidence, patterns and experiences of carers (for example Twigg, 1992; Allen and Perkins, 1995).

During the early 1980s there was a strong sense in the literature that community care was family care and that family care meant care by women (Finch and Groves, 1983). A number of studies of small samples seemed to confirm this picture (Lewis and Meredith, 1988; Ungerson, 1987).

The 1985 General Household Survey was the first large-scale study to include detailed information on Britain's carers. The results of the survey were published in 1988 in a report called *Informal Carers* (Green, 1988). The data, which was obtained from a nationally representative sample of 18 500 adults, indicated that there were about six million carers in Britain: 3.5 million women and 2.5 million men. The data generated a debate on 'who does the caring'. In particular it raised the issue of men as carers because the percentage of male carers (12 per cent of men aged 16 and over were carers) was not a great deal lower than that for women as carers (15 per cent). This seemed to contradict much of the feminist writing on the issue. However the statistics provided a simplified picture. In a re-analysis of the data it was shown that men were less likely to be the 'main' carer, were more likely to be devoting fewer than 20 hours a week to the task and were less likely to be involved in personal caring (Parker and Lawton, 1994).

These overall figures were confirmed by an analysis of 2 700 adult informal carers from the 1990–91 General Household Survey by Arber and Ginn (1995), who found that 10 per cent of men, compared with 13 per cent of women, were involved in some form of caring. Their analysis shows that:

- Men's caring contribution is substantial – especially in later life when men often care for their partner and unmarried men care for a parent within the same household.
- Men are less likely than women to provide care for someone in another household.
- Men carers undertake fewer hours of care each week.
- Men carers are less likely to be the main carer.

The question of caring and gender appears to be less clear-cut than was often claimed during the 1980s. Gender is nevertheless an important variable and Dalley (1996, p. 13) has summarised this as 'Women tended to do more, more often and more intimately'.

In 1999 the government estimated that there were 5.7 million carers in Britain, 58 per cent of whom were women and 42 per cent of whom were men. Nine out of ten carers cared for a relative, with two out of ten caring for a partner or spouse and four out of ten caring for parents. Of the 5.7 million, 1.7 million were estimated to devote at least 20 hours a week to caring, and of those 855 000 did so for 50 hours or more (DoH, 1999a).

There are carers for all of the service user groups, including old people, disabled people, people who are dying, people with drug or alcohol abuse problems, people who have had a stroke, people with dementia, people with learning difficulties and people with mental health problems. Whilst there are common features of caring in all these situations there are also distinctive aspects in terms of the particular reasons why caring is taking place.

In recent years attention has been given to the presence and the needs of young carers. It is not known exactly how many young carers there are in Britain, but research suggests a figure of between 20 000 and 50 000 (DoH, 1999a). There are now a number of projects around the country devoted to meeting the needs of young carers, mostly run by the voluntary sector. The Carers (Recognition and Services) Act 1995 gave particular mention to young carers. They, along with adult carers, have to be assessed for their ability to provide or continue to provide care. Under the Children Act 1989 and the Children (Scotland) Act 1995 a range of services can be provided to children in 'need' and the government has made clear that young carers with significant caring responsibilities can be seen as children in need (CI(95)12).

There is little published material on gay or lesbian carers, but as roughly 10 per cent of the population are gay or lesbian there is bound to be a proportion of gay and lesbian carers in the population who provide care for their partners. Box 2.3 lists a number of the issues for workers and agencies that might arise from the need to provide services for gay and lesbian carers.

Box 2.3   *Developing services for gay and lesbian service users*

- In the light of discrimination and homophobia, how reluctant would the carers be to seek help? What steps could be taken to overcome this fear of discrimination and hostility?
- What should the publicity material of an agency say about its services to gay and lesbian carers?
- What would an equal opportunities policy look like in relation to gay and lesbian service users, and should special mention be made of gay and lesbian carers?
- In reality, how sensitive would the formal services be? What constitutes a sensitive service?
- Heterosexual workers may be discriminatory in attitude. What training would be appropriate for them?

The General Household Surveys have too small a sample of black and ethnic minority carers for any useful analysis. Whilst care giving within the white community has received attention in recent years it remains largely invisible in black and ethnic minority communities (Atkin and Rollings, 1993). There is an assumption that 'they look after their own' and that policy and service provision are equally appropriate for everyone (ibid.) In an overview of the literature Atkin and Rollings (1996, p. 78) argue that when caring responsibilities are taken on, the locus of care is usually the immediate family and the main responsibility falls on one family member, usually the woman. In this respect they note that 'Asian and Afro-Caribbean families are no different from white families' (ibid.) Likewise they argue that 'the experience of care-giving among Asian and Afro-Caribbean carers is broadly similar to that of white people. The physical, emotional and financial consequences of caregiving affect all carers, irrespective of ethnic origin' (ibid., p. 85).

■ Why people do the caring

Community care is a phrase which may conjure up images of a warm, concerned community. In reality community care often means heavy pressures on one relative, often a female relative. This section explores why the relative does the caring and the motivations of love, duty and obligation.

There is no easy answer to why people engage in the care of others as there is a complex of motivating factors. The issue of gender has been much explored in the literature. According to Dalley (1996), women are pushed into 'caring about' and 'caring for' whilst it is acceptable for men just to 'care about'. Dalley argues that 'the whole of community care policies can be seen to be based on the supposition that women are naturally carers, while men are naturally providers' (ibid., p. 18). The altruism of women is presumed upon.

Coresidency and marital relationship (whether male or female) are clearly also important factors in determining the pattern of caring (Parker and Lawton, 1994; Qureshi and Walker, 1989; Finch and Mason, 1993). Social divisions are also relevant when considering the motivation and role of carers – for example class, age, race and sexuality (Sharkey, 1995; Heron, 1998).

Approximately four out of five carers are family members (Green, 1988), and it is clear that family care underpins community care, regardless of ethnic background (Finch, 1989; Atkin and Rollings, 1993). This raises a range of interesting questions, such as how it is decided within families who should care, how much the caring is shared and the nature of the caring.

People's sense of duty and obligation towards their relations helps to sustain them during the process of caring. At the same time their sense of obligation varies according to the situation and their circumstances. Whether the family will care, who within the family will care and how much care will be provided are all sensitive issues and need careful exploration. The message from research for practitioners is that factors such as altruism, obligation and duty make the issue of caring very complicated to untangle (Finch, 1989; Qureshi and Walker, 1989; Finch and Mason, 1993).

Finch, in her study *Family Obligation and Social Change* (1989), makes a number of interesting observations in this respect. She argues that help and support from relatives is based on duty and obligation: 'The idea that kin support is founded, in whole or in part, upon duty and obligation, implies that there is "something special" about social relationships which we have with kin, which makes them distinctively different from all other relationships' (ibid., p. 212).

If kin relationships are special, what is it that is distinctive about them? Finch looks at possible explanations and concludes that the distinctive feature of kin relationships is the question of morality, which puts relationships with kin on a different basis from those with other people (ibid., 1989, p. 236). She argues that four main principles determine who offers personal care (ibid., pp. 27–8):

• The marriage relationship is the most important and the spouse is a prime source of support.
• Second to the marriage relationship is the parent–child relationship.
• People who share the same household are often major sources of support. These often belong to the first two groups. This means that a child who continues to live at home is more likely to be seen as responsible for care than those who have moved away.
• Women are much more likely than men to provide personal care.

The following is the commonly assumed hierarchy of who should care, listed in order of importance (Qureshi and Walker, 1989, p. 126):

• Spouse
• Relative in lifelong joint household
• Daughter
• Daughter-in-law
• Son
• Other relative
• Non-relative

Whilst the influence of duty and obligation is stressed, it is never simple. Finch (1989, ch. 5) argues that support within families cannot be understood just in terms of certain expectations of duty or obligation. When people give support and assistance to their relatives they are not simply acting in accordance with pre-ordained rules, but are engaged in a process of actively working out what to do (ibid., p. 179). Some carers may have a clear idea of what they want to do and what they should do. For others there may be uncertainty, anxiety, hesitation and confusion. Practitioners should bear in mind the varied feelings that might be present. Good counselling skills may be appropriate to help them determine what they can do.

This idea of 'working things out' and 'negotiation' is developed further in *Negotiating Family Responsibilities* by Finch and Mason (1993). The authors argue that relatives do not engage in caring because of fixed rules of obligation or fixed ideas of duty, but rather as a result of complex processes of negotiation. What relatives do in terms of caring depends on relationships within families over time. A history of reciprocity and exchange is the most important factor in creating a sense of obligation. Thus family history and biography interact, resulting in the development of commitment.

Finch and Mason argue that reciprocity is important, and central to their discussion of how reciprocity operates in practice is the concept of 'balance': 'Getting the balance right is a central part of negotiating responsibilities and commitments within kin groups' (ibid., p. 37). There are subtle processes of negotiation and adaptation between parties, and they strive to achieve a balance between offering help and having to ask for it.

The above are brief summaries of complex studies, but some lessons for practitioners can still be drawn:

- Be conscious of the likely hierarchy of obligations.
- Caring responsibilities will probably have been negotiated over time. Be sensitive to this and the history of their development.
- Caring relationships can often be delicate and fragile arrangements and it is important to tread carefully, but there may be times when counselling skills and facilitating family group meetings may be appropriate.

Finch and Mason (1993) note similarities between Asian and white respondents in respect of norms of social obligation. Ahmad (1996) notes the limited literature on family obligations in minority ethnic communities. He draws together some of the available literature and argues that there is a pattern of negotiation based on personal and moral identity, the history of the relationship, the closeness of ties, class, gender and place in the family hierarchy. He notes that there exists a common stereotype of the virtuous caring family, especially the Asian family, but argues that 'These stereotypes ignore both the diversity of perspectives and behaviour within an ethnic group and the similarities across ethnic groups' (ibid., p. 51).

Ahmad stresses the need for more research in this area. He notes the system of obligation and reciprocity that is central to the migration process. In addition to the family itself Ahmad refers to the *biraderi* (a wider kinship-based network where reciprocal relationships are based on moral, financial and social obligation), which is an important source of identity and support (ibid., p. 55). Kin and *biraderi* networks have been important in both the immigration process and the settlement/employment process.

■ Caring is complex

The previous section looked at caring in terms of how kinship rules are negotiated. Nolan *et al.* (1996) stress that caring is a complicated activity and involves much more than practical tasks. People anticipate what may be needed, for example, or monitor vulnerable members of their family at a distance. These activities are elements of caring although not necessarily practical in nature. This complexity needs to be recognised and acknowledged if good practice by practitioners is to emerge.

Nolan *et al.* (ibid.) suggest that interventions can be seen along a continuum ranging from facilitative to obstructive. The intention of the partnership is to facilitate the best outcome for both carer and cared-for. They write that the key determinant of successful facilitative intervention is that 'services are planned in conjunction with the carer and cared-for person to complement their needs. Such services are, unfortunately, not the norm' (ibid., p. 49).

There needs to be a partnership between carer and professional – they should complement each other and the professional may well have much to learn from the carer. Too often help is seen in practical and instrumental terms when there is a need for practitioners to be skilled at dealing with emotions such as loss, grief, anxiety, anger and resentment. These are some of the traditional human relationship skills of social work (often used by all community care workers) and there is an important role for them in community care.

Stress is often a central part of the carer's experience and different people have different abilities to cope with it. It is important for the assessor to try to understand the particular stressors affecting a carer. Nolan *et al.* point out that often the main criteria determining perceived stress are the instrumental aspects of caring. They argue, however, that other factors are more important – such as the nature and quality of relationship, the range of behaviours from the cared-for person and the adequacy of financial resources. The message here for practitioners in respect of assessment is not simply to focus on the practical tasks of personal and domestic care but to include these other factors. Some ideas on this are contained in Box 2.4:

Box 2.4   Developing support for carers

Practitioners can help carers to cope by:
• Identifying and reinforcing appropriate coping responses by the carer.
• Identifying and seeking to reduce inappropriate coping responses.

> • Helping carers to develop new coping resources/responses.
> • Augmenting existing coping resources by building larger support networks.
>
> Nolan *et al.* argue that services should substitute for carers only when the above interventions prove unsuccessful. They also argue that practitioners should adopt a more enabling role by working with carers as partners in ways that are sensitive to the carers' expertise (Nolan *et al.*, 1996, p. 80).

Whilst caring can be stressful there is satisfaction to be gained from the caring role. The obvious point here for the practitioner is that minimising the stress and helping to maximise the satisfaction is important when thinking about intervention (ibid., p. 106).

The complexity of life history, of negotiated caring (Finch and Mason, 1993) and the varied stresses and satisfactions make any assessment time-consuming and require detailed attention to the family's history. Nolan *et al.* (1996) devote a chapter to the way in which caring can go through a series of stages. These stages they describe as building on the past; recognising the need; taking it on; working it through; reaching the end and a new beginning.

■ The tensions between a focus on carers and a focus on independent living

So far this chapter has focused on carers, but it is essential to consider the importance of cared-for persons being responsible for their own lives. Policies and practice that directly try to support, help and maintain family care may run counter to policies and practices that enable people to control their own lives and live independently. This issue was touched on in the case study in Box 2.1 earlier in the chapter and the subsequent discussion, where models 3 and 4 were applied to a young man trying to achieve independence. A theme stressed in writings on disability and dependence is the need for and ability of disabled people to control their own activities, environments and lives. This has perhaps been best articulated by Jenny Morris (1993) in relation to carers of disabled people.

Morris argues that by the end of the 1980s the interests of the disability movement and the Carers National Association were in deep conflict with each other. She writes that 'The identification of informal carers as a social group with specific interests, accompanied as it has been by the social construction of the older and disabled people as "dependent", has tended to limit the opportunities for the interests of older and disabled people to be heard' (ibid., p. 37).

At the heart of her argument is the idea that policy and practice should not endorse dependence by focusing on the support of carers but rather should help disabled people to live independently in the community. The emphasis on carers may divert attention and resources away from this ideal. Morris decries the fact that the voice of the user is absent in the carers' movement and in much of the feminist writing on carers, which stresses the pressure on and oppression of carers. She argues that it is most important not to forget the civil and human rights of older people and disabled people. Likewise Arber and Ginn (1991) argued that there is a great need for policies that recognise older people's rights as citizens and the contribution they have made and still make to society.

Whilst support for carers is important, there is a strong case for arguing that the priority of policy and practice needs to be geared towards achieving and maintaining the independence of older and disabled people. This includes welfare benefits, where hard choices might have to be made between increasing benefits to carers (such as the invalid carer allowance) or providing extra funds to disabled people to enable them to live independently. This is an interesting area where policy and practice may at times conflict and choices have to be made. An appropriate balance is needed between the needs of carers and the achievement of rights for disabled people and older people. This subject will be returned to in Chapter 7.

■ Carers and assessment

The Carers Act 1995 gave carers the right to assessment but it created no right to services. The aim was to bring together the needs identified in two assessments (the section 47 assessment of NH&SCC Act 1990 and the Carers Act 1995) into one care plan. The two key elements of the 1995 Act were the carer's right to ask for an assessment of their ability to care and the local authority's duty to take into account the results of this assessment when looking at what support to provide for the person cared for.

Under the 1995 legislation carers who are engaged in substantial and regular caring (about 20 hours a week or more) have to be informed about their right to be assessed. These assessments may be conducted in the presence or absence of the service user. Carers should be told that, if they wish, their assessment can take place during a separate interview. Indeed it is normally best to assume that this will be the case as there are a number of situations in which it would be preferable and sensible (Heron, 1998, p. 68). Conflicts of interests may emerge from the two assessments and the practitioner may be involved in negotiating around these differing positions.

Heron suggests a framework for a carer assessment. As with any assessment it is important to set carers at ease with some conversation or general open-ended questions, such as 'Could you tell me about the situation as you see it?' or 'Could you explain about any difficulties you are facing?' (ibid., p. 72). The assessors would then explore the carers' responsibilities in terms of what sort of tasks they perform, how often they are required to do them and how long they take. It is important to ascertain how much support is currently being provided, who provides it and how regular and frequent it is. There may also be other people who could help with the caring but are not currently doing so. An assessment would explore the carers' other commitments and the impact of the caring on their lives. Once well settled into the interview the issue should be broached of the carers' relationship with those person being cared for. Heron notes that 'In many cases this issue will be the crux of why they have requested a separate assessment' (ibid., p. 74). An exploration of the carers' expertise and strengths might be followed by an investigation of the support they are looking for and how they feel about caring and the future. The final stage of the assessment is designing a care plan for the user that takes account of the needs of the carer. Any care plan should detail the input by informal carers and a copy should be given to the user and the carer(s).

Sensitivity is important when assessing carers from black or ethnic minority families. This may mean allowing more time in order to minimise the possibility of misunderstandings. If there are language differences, it may be necessary to arrange for an interpreter.

Practitioners may tend to relate people's caring situations to situations of which they have had some personal experience. There is a danger here of over-identification, where practitioners assume that carers have similar feelings and emotions to ones they have had. On the other hand practitioners may overlook some aspects of caring because they have not encountered them before, for example caring in a gay or lesbian relationship or where a young person is caring for an adult.

Assessments are often made on gender-based assumptions. If resources are scarce there may be a tendency (consciously or unconsciously) to base decisions on certain assumptions about who should care. Awareness of the 'hierarchy of obligation' discussed in this chapter may help to avoid sexist assumptions about what a spouse, son or daughter will do. Assessment of caring situations needs to be as free as possible from such assumptions.

In terms of anti-sexist practice, practitioners should try to identify their own assumptions and stereotypes and not base their practice on them. They should not assume that female relatives do the caring and that male relatives do little, and neither the males for the females should be given that impression. An anti-sexist approach involves men changing and doing more caring. It also involves assessors not bending over backwards to help male carers whilst ignoring the real needs of female carers.

■ Practice issues

Information relevant to practice has been threaded throughout the discussion in this chapter but some additional points can be drawn out.

Carers share many concerns and facilitating their coming together is often very helpful. This requires group work and community work skills. Practitioners should find out what local caring groups exist in their area and take the time to learn what they do or ask permission to sit in on one of their meetings. They may be in a position to facilitate links between carers they know and these groups. Where there are no groups they may be able to help set one up.

Each local authority has a community care plan and practitioners should be aware of what the plan for their area says about carers. They should consider whether the policy and strategy towards carers is soundly based and whether carer groups (and other user groups) have had a say in its construction.

Caring is a delicate, sensitive area involving the expression of love, duty and obligation. There may also be pain, hurt and resentment. This chapter has tried to illustrate the complexity of caring and practitioners should remind themselves of this complexity and be sensitive to cues about the nature of caring relationships.

The community care system is bewildering to those who are encountering it for the first time. Practitioners need to provide relevant information and help guide people through it. A number of organisations (for example Age Concern and the Carers National Association) provide help, advice and useful literature. Carers with particular needs can be directed to appropriate sources of information and help. Research has shown the importance to carers of accurate and timely information, but NHS staff have been poor at providing basic information (Henwood, 1998).

In terms of services, respite care is one of the services that carers highly appreciate. There are also a number of carers' centres around the country (Heron, 1998, p. 96) where face-to-face contact with a worker or other carers can help them to develop personal strategies and skills to cope with their problems. Incontinence, for example, can be very stressful for carers but health authorities have incontinence advisers whose practical help and advice can help make the situation much more manageable.

Heron (ibid., p. 59) summarises the main areas where carers require support or service provision as break-taking, practical support, information, training in caring skills, emotional support, problem solving, effective communication, stress management and involvement in the planning and development of services. The first two relate to service provision and the rest to face-to-face work, which might involve individual work, group work or family work.

A range of practitioner skills are needed when working with carers and Heron goes into this in some detail, covering groupwork theory, communication skills training, problem solving and mediation and the applicability of these to carers. She also looks at the different ways in which emotional support and information can be provided.

Later chapters in this book will cover topics that are pertinent to practice with carers, in particular the chapters on social support (Chapter 6), assessment and care management (Chapter 4), user empowerment (Chapter 7) and adult abuse (Chapter 8).

☐ *Further reading*

DoH, *Caring About Carers* (London: DoH 1999). This is the national strategy on carers and draws together data on carers as well as outlining what the government felt was needed in terms of a strategy. It is also available at the web site shown below.

C. Heron, *Working With Carers* (London: Jessica Kingsley, 1998). As the title suggests this is a book for practitioners. It discusses assessment and intervention skills that can be used with carers.

J. Twigg and K. Atkin, *Carers Perceived* (Buckingham: Open University Press, 1994). This book explores how social workers, community nurses and doctors respond to carers and provides an overview of many of the issues concerning carers.

The following books (which have been drawn on in this chapter) contain thought-provoking material on caregiving within families:

J. Finch, *Family Obligation and Social Change* (Cambridge: Polity Press, 1989).

J. Finch and J. Mason, *Negotiating Family Responsibilities* (London: Routledge, 1993).

M. Nolan, G. Grant and J. Keady, *Understanding Family Care* (Buckingham: Open University Press, 1996).

☐ *World Wide Web sites*

Age Concern's site has many pages on matters to do with older people and ageing, including issues relating to caring and carers:

http://www.ace.org.uk

The government's 1999 National Carers Strategy, 'Caring for Carers', can be viewed at

http://www.doh.gov.uk/pub/docs/doh/care.pdf

■ *Chapter 3* ■

The Shifting Boundaries of Community Care

Chapter summary
This chapter: • Presents an overview of the key providers of community care from the formal sector. • Discusses the way in which the boundaries between these key providers have been changing. • Places particular emphasis on the changing boundaries between health and social care.

■ Introduction

Chapter 1 introduced the community care provision by social care agencies and health care agencies. Different agencies and large numbers of people are involved in the various aspects of community care. Service users frequently find this very confusing and require 'help through the maze', as a 1998 White Paper described it (DoH, 1998a, p. 29). Chapter 2 looked in some depth at the contribution made by the informal sector, especially the family. Box 3.1 shows the key providers of community care in the formal sector:

Box 3.1   The formal sector – key providers of community care
• The independent sector   • Housing providers • Statutory social care   • Benefits agencies • Statutory health care   • Private insurance schemes

This chapter will focus on these key providers, with particular emphasis on the long-term care of older people. It is possible to question the composition of this list and argue, for example, that employment and education services should be present. This would especially apply if the focus of our discussion was on disabled people (Bass and Drewett, 1997).

The words 'from the cradle to the grave' are synonymous with Beveridge and everything his 1942 report stood for in terms of social welfare and health care. In recent years there have been substantial boundary changes in social care and health provision that have given substance to the feeling that the 'cradle to grave' promise has been broken. The long-term care of older people is one area where these changing boundaries have been most noticeable and this raises interesting issues of policy and practice. It is also an area where health and social care workers frequently offer advice and guidance so it is important to be aware of the issues and engage in the debate on how society should organise and finance long-term care. In this chapter there will be a particular emphasis on the boundaries between health and social care, but within the context of shifting boundaries in other sectors.

Some significant shifts have been and still are taking place in relation to who should pay for long-term care and the right balance between the state and the individual. Take the example of a man who has received health care in hospital following a stroke. An assessment is conducted and it is decided that he will not be able to live at home. He may well be discharged into a nursing or residential home. After a financial assessment he may have to pay a considerable amount from his savings – perhaps £350 per week for nursing home care or £250 per week for residential care. At the time of writing (1999) if he has more than £16 000 in savings or assets (that is, property) he will have to pay the full cost of this care. If he has less than £10 000 in savings and assets the local authority will pay the fees. With savings/assets of between £10 000 and £16 000 a sliding scale operates. If he has his own house and lives alone, then the house must be sold and the proceeds used to pay for his care. Many people have felt angry and cheated by this, feeling that the 'cradle to grave' care they had been promised, and they believed they had contributed towards financially, has not been honoured. Distress has also been caused by the loss of the heritage they wished to pass on to their children and others. When setting up the welfare state a distinction was made between free services and means-tested services. The National Health Services Act 1946 introduced free care for sick people on a universal basis, regardless of their ability to pay. The National Assistance Act 1948 provided for the local care for older people who needed sheltered or residential accommodation, subject to a means-test. Hence the contrasting systems of means-tested social care and free health care were set up at this stage.

The principle of 'cradle to grave' entitlement regardless of income or assets was applied to health, education, sickness benefit and contributory benefits such as unemployment benefit and the state pension. It was not applied to long-term social care. The NHS was made responsible for sick and infirm older people, providing a free service at the point of delivery, while the long-term social care of older people became the responsibility of local government and was means-tested. Since the start, therefore, 'cradle to grave' care has never been free from payment, although many have perceived it as such. It is not the principle that has changed but rather there has been a dramatic shift in boundaries.

This chapter will now consider in turn each of the providers listed in Box 3.1. During the 1980s there was a continuous reduction in long-term hospital provision for older people. We have seen how expenditure by the Department of Social Security on long-term care increased at a very rapid rate, leading to the expansion of the independent sector. In the 1990s a leading role was given to social service authorities in community care, the independent sector continued to expand and NHS services in the area of long-term community care suffered on-going retrenchment. It is obvious that housing providers are central to successful community care, although recognition of this has been slow to develop. This also applies to benefits agencies. Many people pay for their own community care services through benefits, income or savings. Private insurance schemes are included in our discussion not because they currently are key providers but because there has been much debate about them and they may become key providers in the future.

■ The independent sector

This sector is made up of voluntary and private organisations such as charities, user-run organisations, small family businesses and large commercial care organisations. The purchaser/provider split was brought in with the community care changes and the independent sector is on the provider side, offering services ranging from residential and day care to various aspects of home care. It provides these services through contracts with the statutory sector. The independent sector has grown considerably and its boundaries have expanded as a result of the community care changes. This has usually been at the expense of provision within the statutory sector.

Major contributors to the independent sector are charity organisations and voluntary organisations. Since the late 1970s there have been a number of reports and inquiries into the role of the voluntary sector, stretching from the Wolfenden Report (1978) to the inquiry set up by the National Council for Voluntary Organisations (NCVO, 1996). The voluntary sector is concerned with a broad range of issues and only a proportion of voluntary organisations are involved in community care. Those that are have had to adjust rapidly to the 'contract culture' through which services are delivered. Relations with social service and health authorities have had to change in order to accommodate this. The emphasis on the development of a 'mixed economy of care' has encouraged the growth of this sector and is based on the belief that competition will improve efficiency and the resulting services will be more cost-effective than the welfare bureaucracies of the past. The reforms mean that the statutory authorities have a responsibility to support and stimulate the market so that a wider choice is available for users. For example in areas such as drug and alcohol misuse and provision for people with HIV/AIDS the majority of provision is by the independent sector, with local authorities and health authorities usually acting as funders and commissioners rather than providers.

In 1998 the private medical insurer Bupa became the UK's biggest provider of residential and nursing homes. Over three quarters of residential accommodation for older and disabled people is provided by the independent sector, much of this by private firms. The sector ranges from very small organisations to very large companies. Since the private residential care sector's boom period in the 1980s (see Chapter 1) occupancy levels have fallen, putting homes under threat. In terms of the changing boundaries in residential/nursing care of older people, key shifts have been the contraction of local authority provision since the early 1980s and the rapid expansion of the independent sector, funded during the 1980s through social security payments. Between 1983 and 1996 there was a 242 per cent increase in residential and nursing home beds in the independent sector whilst the number of residential beds in local authority facilities fell by 43 per cent (Audit Commission, 1997, p.10). This was a big boundary shift in a short number of years.

In the late 1990s there was a continuing decline in local authority provision but a levelling off of the expansion of the independent sector. The change of funding from open-ended income support to funding through the cash-limited social service authorities' budgets had the effect of curtailing the expansion and reducing the profits of the private sector. The introduction of the minimum wage has also affected cost, fee and profit levels. The 'market-place' of homes has resulted in many takeovers, mergers, sales and closures, creating instability and insecurity for residents. The future is likely to see further closures and diversification into other areas, especially providing for the 'self-paying' care market.

The shift to what is usually called the 'mixed economy of care' was a conscious government policy and, as noted in Chapter 1, 85 per cent of the Special Transitional Grant over the first four years had to be spent on care provided by the independent sector.

■ Social care

Under the NHS&CC Act 1990 social service authorities were given the lead role in the coordination of community care and the development of care management. The Act changed the financial and management structures under which care and support were provided and this involved considerable changes within social service authorities. After the implementation of the Act, people could not go into residential or nursing home care paid for by the state without an assessment coordinated by the social service authority. Hence social service authorities came to have a crucial gate-keeping role.

Chapter 1 noted that the funds that had been coming through social security payments were capped and transferred to local authorities through the STG, in addition to the money coming through their Standard Spending Assessment (SSA). The actual baseline SSA between 1993 and 1996 increased by only 1 per cent (Audit Commission, 1997, p. 45). Many authorities really had to struggle to provide services within their limited resources.

This was a dramatic change in the role of social service authorities and social workers. Agency and individual responsibilities increased as they had to take over some of the responsibilities of the Benefits Agency and the National Health Service. During the 1990s social service authorities considerably reduced their own provision of residential care, focused (through eligibility criteria) on those most in need of services and took on financial assessments and charging to a much greater extent.

In the first year of operation quite generous packages of care could be afforded, but money then became much tighter and social service authorities had to reduce their spending and tighten their eligibility criteria. What emerged was considerable variation in assessment, eligibility criteria and charging, leading to a lottery of care in the sense that service users in exactly the same situation could receive a very different level of services and have very different charges depending on the area in which they lived (DoH, 1998a).

The figures below show the distribution of social service authority money for the 75-plus age group in England. As can be seen, nearly two thirds (64 per cent) of expenditure goes on residential and nursing home care (Audit Commission, 1997, p. 34):

• Residential care: 46 per cent.
• Nursing home care: 18 per cent.
• Home care: 28 per cent.
• Day centres: 5 per cent.
• Meals: 3 per cent.

With the contraction of NHS responsibilities social service authorities have been subjected to considerable extra pressure due to the volume of NHS referrals. This has sometimes been portrayed by NHS managers and the media as 'bed-blocking'. The authorities have in a sense increased their responsibilities and costs through having a lead role, but they have lost much of their direct provision to the independent sector through the growth of the mixed economy and often act as an intermediary between these two powerful sectors. As the Audit Commission (1997, p. 15) has noted, 'Placed centrally between the NHS and independent sectors, social services encounter dissiculties at both these interfaces.'

A further shift of roles and boundaries came with the Community Care

(Direct Payments) Act 1996, through which social service authorities could become income maintenance agencies by making direct cash provision. In the past cash was provided by the social security system, so here was another shift in boundaries. Some commentators believe that this role of cash provision will expand (Becker, 1997).

Thus there have been shifting responsibilities and shifting boundaries for social service authorities in respect of the community care changes. Whilst the direct provision of services by them has decreased, they have taken on a lead role, increased their overall budgets and been far more involved in commissioning services from agencies in the independent sector. They have also taken on an income maintenance role.

■ Health care

Chapter 1 referred to some of the changing boundaries within the health service, notably the prioritisation of primary care and increased attention given to preventive health. There has been a considerable shift of personal care provision away from district nurses towards social service authorities (Audit Commission, 1999). However it has been the contraction of continuing long-term care within the health service that has had the most impact on the social care services, causing tension and problems between health services and social service authorities.

There was a 38 per cent reduction in acute and long-stay beds in the NHS for older people between 1983 and 1996 and an almost ninefold increase in beds in independent nursing homes (Audit Commission, 1997, p. 12). This represents a very considerable shift of care from free NHS care to means-tested social care. The NHS's shift of emphasis towards acute care, defining everything else as 'social care', has generated a considerable amount of concern and discussion.

A circular issued in 1989 (HC(89)5) made clear that no NHS patients could be transferred to a private nursing home against their wishes if they or their family were then liable to pay for part or all of the fees (Richards, 1996, p. xi). The case that triggered changes is described in Box 3.2.

Box 3.2   Mr X and Leeds Health Authority
A fifty-five year old Mr X was treated at Leeds General Infirmary after a double brain haemorrhage. He was doubly incontinent and could not walk, feed himself or communicate. He also had a kidney tumour, cataracts in both eyes and suffered epileptic fits. The hospital insisted on his discharge in 1991 on the ground that nothing more could be done for him. He was then sent to a private nursing home. The cost of the nursing home was about £340 a week, and his family had to meet the shortfall of more than £6 000 a year between his income support benefits and the home's fees. Mr X's wife complained to

the Health Service Commissioner, who ruled in her favour and said the hospital should compensate the family and meet all future costs of Mr X's care. The Leeds Health Authority's policy was to make no provision for continuing care at NHS expense either in hospital or in private nursing homes. However the Commissioner ruled that someone such as Mr X, requiring full nursing care, was indeed the responsibility of the National Health Service (Health Service Commissioner, 1994).

The Health Service Commissioner (1994) selected Mr X's case from a number of similar complaints as an example of a general problem. He sought to ensure that the significance of his findings were not diluted by taking the unprecedented step of devoting a whole report to a single case. It had the effect he intended as the government was forced to acknowledge that the NHS had withdrawn too far from its responsibilities for long-term, continuing care.

It was clear that there were serious problems over financial responsibility, with the NHS apparently trying to redefine aspects of health care as social care. The government responded by issuing a guidance document in February, 1995, entitled *NHS Responsibilities for Meeting Continuing Health Care Needs* (LAC (95)5). In this guidance patients kept the right to refuse to leave hospital for means-tested residential care. However if they did refuse they might be sent home with a package of community care services, towards which they would have to pay. This would be 'within the options and resources available' (ibid.)

The impetus for the development of eligibility criteria for continuing care had come from the Leeds case, and LAC(95)5 was an attempt to clarify what the health service was actually responsible for in terms of continuing care. The document spelt out this responsibility only in broad terms, covering specialist clinical supervision in hospitals and nursing homes, rehabilitation, palliative health care, respite health care, community health services support and specialist health care support in different settings. The detail was left for health authorities to sort out in consultation at the local level. The boundaries were shifting but they were shifting in different ways at the local level.

Health authorities had to review their continuing care arrangements, and where gaps in provision were identified they had to put this right with future investment plans. Not all local authorities signed up to their local continuing care plan so a number were not agreed. Palliative care is one area where there has been some dispute. One health authority said it would pay for those who were predicted to have just one month to live, whereas the local authority felt the period should be three months. In another area the health authority was providing little or no respite care. Service users in that area did not have the option of, for example, free health authority respite care every two weeks in six and so they had to go into a nursing home paid for by themselves and the social service authority.

Hence the health authority saved some money at considerable cost to the individual service users and the social service authority.

The government avoided giving clear guidance on this and stressed the importance of 'local criteria'. Government ministers emphasised that it was up to doctors to decide when health care finished and social care started. In practice, this can often be as difficult a distinction for doctors to make as it is for anyone else. Doctors are not experts on social care and the concepts of health and social care are inherently contested and contestable. John Bowis, a government minister at the time, was given the example of somebody on a drip, doubly incontinent, relatively helpless and requiring a lot of nursing care. Even with this deliberately extreme example he would not concur that this person was clearly on the health side of the divide (HoC, 1995, vol. 2, p. 23).

The LAC(95)5 guidance provided a safeguard against the arbitrary or inconsistent operation of procedures through the right to ask the health authority to review individual cases 'as a final check before such discharge is implemented' (ibid., para. 30). The 'normal expectation' is for the health authority to seek the advice of independent panels in such cases. Although these panels have no legal status and their decisions are not formally binding, 'the expectation would be that [their] recommendation would be accepted in all but very exceptional circumstances' (ibid., para. 33). The panels' key task is to assess whether the health authority's eligibility criteria have been correctly applied and hence they are required to review the clinical judgements of the professionals concerned. To this end they have access to independent clinical advice.

The health and social service authorities have often found it difficult to adjust to the changes expected of them and change previous patterns of expenditure in order to develop more appropriate services (Audit Commission, 1997, p. 39). Often, plans for the development of community care services (for example 'hospital at home' schemes or intensive domiciliary care schemes) have been hindered. The Audit Commission has noted that a range of pressures have curtailed the development of better balanced services and made working together more difficult. These are shown in Box 3.3.

> ### Box 3.3   *Pressures hindering better balanced services –*
> *a vicious circle*

On the NHS side the pressures have been:

- The rise in the rate of emergency admissions.
- Pressure to reduce the lengths of stay.
- Insufficient 'intermediate' options between acute and long-term care.

On the side of the social service authorities the pressures have been:

- Pressure to place service users in nursing and residential homes.
- Lower priority given to alternative services in the community.
- Limits on the number of placements.

According to the Audit Commission, these pressures on the NHS and social service authorities are combining to create a vicious circle. 'The pressure on expensive hospital beds and the high use of residential and nursing homes is making it hard to free up resources for alternative services that might start to ease the situation' (ibid., p. 50). The Commission argues that joint planning and joint commissioning are essential if this vicious circle is to be broken.

Debates on and concern about who should provide and who should pay underlie many of the frustrations of practitioners in this area. It was also a central concern of the Royal Commission on Long Term Care, which reported in early 1999. We shall look at its recommendations towards the end of the chapter.

So far consideration has been given to the contribution of the informal sector (Chapter 2), the independent sector, the social care sector and the health sector and the way in which their boundaries have been changing in respect of community care for older people. Consideration will now be given to the role of housing in community care.

■ Housing

In comparison with health and social care provision, housing provision has received relatively little attention in the discussion of community care. The choice for older people is not a stark one of staying in their own home or going into a nursing/residential home. There are a range of options in between and there could and should be more. Organisations for disabled people have often argued that 'the disabling society' prevents people from living to their full potential and housing provision is often an element of this. Houses and flats can be adapted to meet changing needs. New technology can be used in various ways to enable people to live more easily and safely in their own homes. There are various types of supported and sheltered housing schemes and some housing associations have developed a range of schemes to meet different needs. Without appropriate housing, community care cannot work.

The Griffiths Report (1988) paid little attention to housing issues but *Caring for People* (DoH, 1989a, p. 3) argued that 'Community care means providing the services and support which people who are affected by problems of ageing, mental illness, mental handicap, or physical or sensory disability need to be able to live as independently as possible in their own homes, or in "homely" settings in the community'. *Caring for People* argued that suitable, good-quality housing is essential to social care pack-ages and that 'social services authorities will need to work closely with housing authorities, housing associations and other providers of housing of all types in developing plans for a full and flexible range of housing' (ibid., p. 25).

The development of plans for independent living requires control not only over support but also over the environment in terms of appropriate housing. This necessitates workers working together across departments and agencies. In the 1990s the discussion on community care concentrated on nursing homes and residential care and far too little attention was paid to other links between housing and community care.

There is a need to open up mainstream housing to community care user groups and there is also a need for appropriate supported housing. Supported housing, where extra help is built into the basic provisions, includes sheltered housing, hostels and shared housing. Supported housing has been used a good deal in the resettlement of people with learning dis-abilities or mental health problems after their discharge from hospital. Sheltered housing for older people is the largest element of supported housing, much of it provided by local authorities. Very sheltered housing, where quite a lot of personal care is available, has been developed by large, specialist housing associations such as Anchor and Hanover. Shared hous-ing has also been promoted by housing associations such as the Abbeyfield Society, the Carr-Gomm Society, the St Matthew Society and the St Mungo Association (Cooper *et al.*, 1994).

In addition most social service authorities have 'adult placement' schemes that operate on a short- or long-term basis. These schemes, which are rather like adult fostering schemes, provide a supported home environ-ment. The boundaries of what may be regarded as residential care are shifting as different options open up. If more appropriate and varied sup-ported housing were to become available, the question could arise of who would really need residential and nursing home care.

Some progress is being made towards housing being viewed as having a central and important role in community care provision, but more is need-ed as housing is fundamental to any community care strategy. The idea of 'normalisation', which underpins much of community care provision, emphasises the aim of integration into the community and of keeping peo-ple in socially valued environments such as ordinary housing, or as near to this as possible. Whilst there has been some government rhetoric about housing being the cornerstone of community care, in practice it seems that housing issues have struggled to be integrated into the community care agenda (Clapham and Franklin, 1994).

This picture was confirmed by an Audit Commission report in 1998. The report examined the performance of housing agencies in identifying social need, adapting properties, providing personal support, offering places in 'special needs' projects, and coordinating services. It outlined the ways in which aspects of housing could take a central place within the overall provision of community care, through, for example, community alarms, aids and adaptations, home improvement agencies, housing the homeless, specialised housing and mainstream housing with support. The Royal Commission on Long Term Care also stressed the centrality of housing, arguing that 'A larger proportion of care than now should be provided in peoples' own homes, either in the houses in which they live or in new settings which are closer to the community and which allow a greater degree of independence than traditional residential or nursing care' (RCLTC, 1999, p. 82). For example owner-occupiers who needs repairs to be done or adaptations made to their houses should have access to easier ways of releasing some of the value of their houses in order to achieve this (ibid., p. 51).

Well-designed housing (and of course all other buildings) can increase independence and release carers from some aspects of personal care. This has been slow to develop, but in early 1998 the government announced that all new housing would have to be accessible to disabled people. This would include features such as level thresholds, wider doorways and ground-floor toilets.

■ Benefits agencies

For those with adequate personal resources and wealth, finding good and effective care is not a problem. People can buy in help for most situations, for example domestic cleaning, night sitting and nursing. For those without personal wealth, social security and welfare benefits crucially underpin the community care programme as they provide for basic essentials such as food, clothing and fuel, as well as helping with housing costs. The availability and delivery of these benefits is often critical to the sort of package of care the social worker or care manager can put together, and indeed can determine whether someone can live independently in the community at all. Thus the boundaries and linkages between the provision of social service authorities and social security provision are very important in discussions of community care.

It is well known that many benefits are not claimed by those who are eligible for them. There are various reasons for this. Potential claimants may not know about them. They may be put off by the complexity of the forms. They may feel too proud to claim. It is certainly a very complicated and cumbersome system. It is very important for people in need of community care to have their full entitlement because poverty can only make their situation worse. If they are at home and are contributing to the cost of services it is obviously crucial for them to have received their full entitlement, and health and social care workers have a part to play in ensuring this happens. Welfare benefits provision is a large and complicated area but it is essential for health and social care workers to have a sound knowledge of it so that the people they are working with can maximise their financial resources. Some published guides to benefits are listed at the end of this chapter. Box 3.4 gives a brief overview of the nature of the benefits available.

Box 3.4   An overview of welfare benefits

Welfare benefits can be divided into three basic categories, and many adults who need community care are entitled to benefits in each of the categories:

- Contributory benefits are based on national insurance contributions paid whilst in work. Examples of such benefits are incapacity benefit and the retirement pension.
- Means-tested benefits are paid irrespective of contributions when income and capital are less than the prescribed levels. Examples are income support and housing benefit. Under this we would include the social fund, through which it is possible to obtain community care grants (intended to promote community care by helping people move out of, or stay out of, institutional or residential care and by assisting families under exceptional pressure).
- Non-contributory benefits are paid irrespective of national insurance contributions and means. Examples that are especially important in relation to community care are the disability living allowance (DLA), attendance allowance (for people over 65) and invalid care allowance for some carers.

It has been noted how during the 1980s the Department of Social Security met some of the costs of long-term care. Older people with limited resources could choose to go into independent homes and have their fees paid by the Department of Social Security. The expenditure in this area increased very rapidly, leading to pressure for the reforms that the NHS&CC Act 1990 introduced in relation to community care. This offered the NHS the opportunity to reduce its long-term care responsibilities and there was a significant boundary shift between the health services and the social security system.

The boundary shifted again in 1993 when social service authorities took over the lead organising and financing role. The role of the Department of Social Security was reduced, although of course it remained substantial. An increasing amount of local authority time was given over to ensuring that people received their full entitlement of social security benefits. Of course social service authorities realised that the more people could pay for themselves the less drain there would be on their limited resources, and research indicates that 37 per cent of claim forms for the DLA and attendance allowance were filled in by social service authorities and allied professionals (LGA, 1997, p. 23). Social care professionals often took on this advisory task before the community care changes, but it now seems to be a greater part of their role and another aspect of the shift in boundaries. The claim forms for the DLA and attendance allowance are lengthy, complicated and off-putting. However, for those who need considerable help if they are to continue to live in the community and maintain their independence, these benefits are crucially important. They can help towards local authority charges, help pay for private care arrangements and help with small adaptations to the home.

The Benefits Agency's Social Fund is inadequate to the task of providing flexible and quick support to enable people to live independently in the community. The Community Care Grants under the Social Fund have a very high refusal rate and a budget that has been held very low, a state of affairs which directly affects the ability of social service authorities to help vulnerable adults to remain in the community.

According to a Local Government Association report in 1997, a large number of vulnerable people in need of financial assistance were going without because they saw the system as impossible to access. This was a result of the Benefits Agency giving priority to anti-fraud initiatives, the complexity of the system and the application process itself. This had obvious implications for social service authorities. The report states that the inability of the Benefits Agency to undertake its work effectively, 'results in many instances in the creation of more clients for SSDs as, for example, people are compelled to seek assistance from social services when the Agency fails to either deliver benefits due on time, or at all' (LGA, 1997, p. 25).

Housing benefit has been very important to people living in supported housing as it helps to cover, for example, alarm and warden provision in sheltered housing. The government has been reviewing this and is planning to move towards a more simplified system of paying for these important supportive services (DSS, 1999).

At the time of writing there is much debate on and argument about the Labour government's plans in relation to benefits for disabled people. The government has tried to counter fears of cutbacks and the withdrawal of benefits by stressing that it intends to provide opportunities for disabled people to find work and come off benefit.

■ Private insurance schemes

Much community care is paid for by the users themselves, either through charges levied by social service authorities or by paying directly for private services. People pay from their current income, their savings, through an annuity on their property or through a private insurance scheme. With the cash-starved plight of social service authorities, means-testing has resulted in many older people meeting all or part of the cost of social care themselves.

It was noted in Chapter 1 that, when allocating money for community care to the local authorities, the government assumes they will raise 9 per cent of the cost of domiciliary services through charges. Because of the financial pressure they are having to bear, local authorities have had little option but to raise this amount through charging. Charging is not new but the services charged for and the amount charged have increased considerably during the 1990s, causing some controversy. The systems for charging are varied and complex (Baldwin, 1997). One aim of the community care changes was to limit expenditure. Shifting the cost of care across to service users themselves helps to achieve this aim.

One way of avoiding paying for future care out of savings and property is to take out a long-term care insurance policy. Private health insurance has become more widespread, but insurance for long-term care has been taken up more slowly. Long-term care policies pay out an income (often after a waiting period of, say, 90 days) if the policy holder becomes unable to cope on her or his own. The income can be used to pay for nursing or residential care, or to pay for help at home. If it is paid directly to a nursing or residential home, the income may be tax-free; in other cases it is usually taxable. Typically these policies pay out if the policy holder becomes 'mentally impaired' or unable to carry out two or three out of five 'activities of daily living': these are usually defined as washing, dressing, feeding oneself, moving around and toileting. Most claims involve an independent assessment of whether the insured person can manage these daily activities by themselves. So far there has been little experience of these policies so it is hard to know if they work, but clearly there is great scope for disagreement about whether or not someone is able to carry out the activities in question.

There are two types of long-term care plan. The first is known as a pre-funded plan and is for people in their forties, fifties or sixties who wish to provide for their future by paying into an insurance policy over a number of years. With these plans the earlier they are entered the less they are likely to cost each month. The second type is called an immediate needs plan and uses a lump sum investment (an annuity) to provide an immediate regular income to pay for private care. According to the Royal Commission on Long Term Care the Commercial Union introduced the first policy in 1991 and by 1999 14 companies were offering policies, with about 23 000 policies in force (RCLTC, 1999, para. 5.2). It was also noted that the growth of the market had been slow.

Before its electoral defeat in 1997 the Conservative government was keen to promote these private insurance schemes and mooted the idea of a 'partnership', whereby the government would encourage people to join such schemes by subsidising them, thus enabling people to pay for their own future social care costs. The proposals were heavily criticised as a middle class prerogative, available only to those who were well-resourced. Progress was in any event halted by the change of government. However they clearly show how the government of the day was trying to shift the social care boundaries.

The majority of the members of the Royal Commission on Long Term Care did not see a central role for private insurance or partnership schemes, although there were two dissenters who did. Until the government decides on a clear way forward, the role of private insurance in long-term care will remain a matter for discussion.

■ Shifting boundaries

There were two key factors underpinning some of the boundary shifts of the 1990s, both of which essentially related to the crucial matter of cost:

- The demographic change in the population in relation to older people.
- The cost of nursing home care and residential care.

First, with the demographic change there is a fear that the huge rise in the population of older people will be very expensive and unmanageable. The population of the UK has been growing throughout the century. With the improvement in life expectancy the number of those aged 65 and over has also been growing, and since 1931 the number of older people has doubled (RCLTC, 1999, p. 13). These trends are projected to continue until about 2030, when overall population growth is expected to level out and the number of those aged 65–84 is expected to fall. However the number of those aged 85 and over is expected to continue to increase beyond 2030, with this group tripling in size between 1999 and 2050 (ibid., p. 14). The Royal Commission on Long Term Care argues that the UK lived through its demographic 'time bomb' earlier in the century and that these future projections are manageable (ibid.)

Concern about the demographic changes links to the cost of nursing home and residential care. This issue was tackled under the NHS&CC Act 1990 by the switch of funding to social service authorities and with the need for social workers to assess people before they could enter residential or nursing home care. As soon as 'free' health treatment was deemed to be unnecessary, people became a cost responsibility of social service authorities, which only had limited budgets. It then became crucial to decide what the dividing line was between health care/treatment and social care. The former was free to the user whilst the second was means-tested.

Earlier in the chapter it was noted how the number of long-term care beds provided by the NHS has declined since the 1980s. For example the number of NHS long-stay beds was reduced by 38 per cent between 1983 and 1999 (a loss of 21 300 beds). Over the same period the number of private nursing home places increased by 38 per cent, with an increase of 141 000 beds (RCLTC, 1999, p. 34). There has been a retrenchment by the NHS in this whole area. Many long-term care wards for older people (free for users) have been closed to save money.

Health managers, all with their own pressures, have also tried to pull back from commitments on community provision. At the local level there has been disagreements over who should provide personal care, for example bathing. Health providers have increasingly withdrawn from this provision and social service authorities have had to pick it up. As MP David Congdon, told the House of Commons Health Committee:

> I think most social services departments up and down the country would say to you that since the early 1980s, not since the community care legislation, but since the early 1980s, NHS managers, trusts, call them what you like, have used any and every opportunity to reduce their provision knowing the burden would fall on the social security budget or on social services (HoC, 1995, vol. 2, p. 22).

The blurred responsibilities between health care providers and social care providers has caused considerable tension. The overall process has involved a push from free NHS care to means-tested local authority care. The biggest and most contentious shift has been the closure of hospital beds and the push towards means-tested long-term care. In the early and mid 1990s the government's strategy seemed to be to demedicalise provision and to define it as social rather than medical care. This had the money-saving benefit of moving it out of the 'cradle to grave' NHS sector and into the means-tested social care sector.

The Labour government set up the Royal Commission on Long Term Care to report on this important topic. In its full report it provided a definition of personal care that cut across the areas of social and health care. Its definition of personal care included all direct care relating to washing, bathing, dressing, skin care, eating, drinking, and urinary/bowel functions, as well as managing problems associated with mobility, the management of prescribed treatment and the management of behaviour and safety, but excluded cleaning, housework, laundry, shopping, specialist transport and sitting services.

The Royal Commission's key recommendation was that individuals should pay for their own living and housing costs (subject to means-testing) but that the state would pay for personal care costs out of general taxation. For example (using some figures drawn from the report), someone in a nursing home costing £337 a week might pay £120 for living and housing costs, with the remaining £217 of personal care costs being paid for out of general taxation. At the time of writing it is not clear whether the government will accept this proposal or regard it as too expensive. The debate goes on. Long-term care can be financed from public finance or private finance or a mixture of both. Private sources include personal savings, housing equity, personal pensions and private insurance. Public sources include increased resources obtained through the tax system or a social insurance scheme (Harding *et al.*, 1996, p. 17).

There are often newspaper headlines about 'bed-blocking' and the issue is invariably expressed simplistically. It is sometimes portrayed as being the fault of ineffective and ineffectual social workers – people are staying in hospital longer than necessary because social workers are too slow to do the assessments and arrange the next stage of care. Because of media coverage and the question of cost-responsibility, long-term continuing care has become one of the most important and contentious issues arising out of the community care changes of the early 1990s.

This chapter has stressed that the key providers of community care experienced a shifting of their boundaries during the late 1980s and the 1990s. Long-term care for older people has been taken as a particular example and it has been noted how there has been a cost-shunting from the NHS to social service authorities. The complexity of it all led to the setting up of a Royal Commission. The topic is a most interesting and important area of social policy, relevant to us all in the future!

As a way of reflecting on the information in this chapter, consider the scenario in Box 3.5.

Box 3.5   Scenario

Joe Brown was self-employed in the building trade. He is now 88 years old. His wife died in July 1995. Since then he has lived alone in a privately owned terraced property, worth about £50 000. He has savings of £55 000. He suffers from arthritis and has a hearing impairment.

He is isolated with few contacts. He has one son who lives 100 miles away and visits only occasionally.

Suddenly Joe has a stroke and is admitted to hospital. He is paralysed down one side and cannot walk. He is doubly incontinent. After a few weeks his medical condition stabilises.

Consider:

• In 1966 what was likely to happen to him next?
• What was the likely outcome in 1996?
• What is the likely outcome if the Royal Commission's proposals on personal care are implemented?

Before reading on, reflect on your answers and on what you have read so far in this chapter. Then have a look some possible responses in Box 3.6.

Box 3.6   Possible responses

Obviously with limited information and regional variations in services there can be no definitive answers. These are some thoughts:

In 1966 the son may well have been seen as someone to whom Joe could go, although the brief description in Box 3.5 does not suggest that this was very likely. With Joe's isolation and limited possibility of support at home, one likely outcome might have been a long-stay hospital, given that there were far more beds at that time. This would of course have been free provision under the NHS.

In 1996 a comprehensive assessment would have been carried out by the social service authority. A likely outcome is that the authority would have decided that he should go into a nursing home at a cost of about £330 a week. His capital would have paid for this at first, followed by the proceeds from the sale of his house (with the social service authority only starting to make a contribution when savings were down to £16 000). Once his savings were below £10 000, Joe would still have contributed to his care through his pension or income support, but his remaining savings would not be used. The social service authority would have paid the remainder of the fees.

If the Royal Commission's proposals on personal care were to be implemented then again a comprehensive assessment would be carried out, with the likely outcome of a placement in a nursing home at a cost of say £350 a week. Joe would pay for his living and housing costs from his pension and/or benefit and from his savings/capital. This would be in the region of £125 per week which might well be covered by his income and interest on his savings.

■ Practice issues

This chapter has discussed the need to know about and work with a variety of organisations. It has pointed to the contribution made by different agencies to community care and the importance of working with people from these agencies. The need for inter-disciplinary working will be discussed further in Chapter 5

Many workers in the NHS and the social service authorities – as well as users and carers – are not aware of the local continuing care criteria (Todhunter, 1998). A first task for practitioners is to find out what they are and the procedures required to access them.

People can refuse to be discharged into a residential or nursing home, although they cannot stay in hospital indefinitely. Patients should be made aware of this so that they are not forced to go somewhere they do not want to go to in order to release a bed.

Patients need to be aware of the review system of eligibility for long-term care. A faxed message from the patient or a carer to the chief executive of the hospital trust should set this in motion and freeze any immediate plans the hospital may have. If, for example, someone was being discharged to a nursing home at her or his own expense and a clinician had said that she or he only had four months to live, a practitioner could look at the local continuing care policy on palliative care and probably challenge this decision by saying it was the responsibility of the trust.

Practitioners need to be aware of and give guidance on complaints procedures within social service authorities and the NHS. They also should note the possibility of users/patients approaching the Health Service Commissioner, who has taken a particular interest in hospital discharges.

It is essential for all community care users to receive their full benefit entitlement, so practitioners need to be able to give sound and effective advice on this matter. Two guides to benefits are included in the list below.

Community care provision is complicated and varied, requiring a large amount of knowledge in order to inform, advise and (where necessary) advocate. Particular emphasis has been given in this chapter to the continuing care criteria and the need for knowledge about welfare benefits, but it is important to be able to give advice in many areas. For example there is often a lack of guidance to prospective residents about choosing a home. A useful guide for users and their carers has been produced by the King's Fund, with background information and checklists on what to look for and ask about (Turnbull, 1998).

☐ *Further reading*

There are a number of useful publications on welfare benefits and long-term care, including the following.

Child Poverty Action Group, *Welfare Benefits Handbook*. This two-volume annual can be purchased from the Child Poverty Action Group, 94 White Lion Street, London, N1 9PF.

Disability Alliance, *Disability Rights Handbook*. Produced annually, this handbook contains a detailed and comprehensive account of benefit rights and services for people with disabilities and their families. It can be purchased from the Disability Alliance, Universal House, 88–94 Wentworth Street, London, E1 7SA.

T. Harding, B. Meredith and G. Wistow *Options for Long-Term Care* (London: HMSO, 1996).

E.Richards *Paying for Long-Term Care* (London: IPPR, 1996). This provides an overview of the current system, estimates the future costs of long-term care, analyses the shortcomings of the present system and considers alternative policy options.

Joseph Rowntree Foundation, *Meeting the Costs of Continuing Care* (York: Joseph Rowntree Foundation, 1996). This calls for free care in old age, backed by compulsory care insurance.

Royal Commission on Long Term Care, *With Respect to Old Age* (London: Stationery Office, 1999) (main report and three volumes of evidence). This document looks fully at the issue and debates and is an obvious choice for further reading.

☐ *World Wide Web site*

The full Royal Commission report, *With Respect to Old Age*, is available at
http://www.open.gov.uk/royal-commission-elderly/

It can be accessed by clicking on 'final report'.

■ *Chapter 4* ■

Care Management and Assessment

Chapter summary

This chapter contains:

- A description of case management.
- Some details on the background of care management.
- A description of assessment within care management.
- An evaluation of the experience of care management.

■ Introduction

The contribution of informal carers was the theme of Chapter 2 and the contribution of formal organisations was covered in Chapter 3. A key part of the community care strategy was that these different contributions (from the formal and informal sector) would be coordinated through care management. In *Caring for People*, there was a particular emphasis on case or care management. In situations where needs were numerous or involved significant expense, 'the Government sees considerable merit in nominating a "case manager" to take responsibility for ensuring that individuals' needs are regularly reviewed, resources are managed effectively and that each service user has a single point of contact' (DoH, 1989a, p. 21).

Caring for People and the subsequent guidance literature stated quite clearly that care management, along with assessment, were to be key elements in the provision of services. In both the managers' and the practitioners' guide to care management the opening statement emphasises that 'Care management and assessment constitutes the core business of arranging care, which underpins all other elements of community care' (DoH, 1991a, p. 7; 1991b, p. 5).

Social service authorities were required to introduce a system of care management from April 1993. However they each did this in different ways and so there are a number of different types of care management and assessment (Lewis and Glennerster, 1996; Davis *et al.*, 1997; Challis, 1999). Within social service authorities, care management has largely been built on the social work culture (Welch, 1998) and the health content of the work has been limited, variable and locally defined. Challis (1999) argues that there is little evidence of health and social services 'jointness' in the arrangements, except in the field of mental health. The Audit Commission (1999, p. 107) argues that in many places the system of care management is a barrier to good teamwork between social services staff and district nurses.

The Department of Health has produced quite detailed advice on care management (DoH, 1991a, 1991b), which is described as the process of tailoring services to individual needs. Seven core tasks are involved in arranging care for someone in need:

- The publication of information.
- Determining the level of assessment.
- Assessing need.
- Care planning.
- Implementing the care plan.
- Monitoring.
- Reviewing.

Stages 3 to 7 are best seen as a cyclical process whereby needs are assessed, services are delivered in response to the identified needs, and the needs are then re-assessed, resulting in the possibility of a changed service response. In this way reviewing can feed back into a re-assessment of the situation and the establishment of a new or revised care plan (DoH, 1991a, 1991b). It is interesting to note that this model does not incorporate the notion of care termination, suggesting that 'vulnerable' people will always require some form of care.

■ A case study of care management

The process of care management and the stages can best be illustrated through a case study. Read first the scenario in Box 4.1.

Box 4.1   A case study

Mary Warwick lives alone in her own terraced house. There is no outstanding mortgage on the house and is valued at about £30 000. Mary is 66 years old and her sole income is her state pension.

Two months ago Mary had a stroke but she is now ready to be discharged from hospital. However the stroke has left her with extremely restricted mobility and she cannot climb stairs without help. The stroke has affected her left side and she cannot use her left arm or hand. She needs help with toiletting, getting dressed, and the laundry. Furthermore her speech is considerably impaired.

Mary is keen to return home but there is concern about her ability to cope. In addition to her need for support services the house will require some adaptations. Mary has one daughter, Sarah, who lives on her own about five miles away and is currently working.

We shall now examine each of the seven stages of care management in order to gain an idea of what each means in relation to this situation.

☐ *Published information*

The local authority has a booklet on care management and during Mary's stay in hospital copies are given to her and her daughter, Sarah, by the hospital social worker, Janet. At appropriate points other published material is made available to them. This might include the health authority's leaflet on continuing care and leaflets on complaints procedures in relation to the hospital trust and the social service authority. All this literature should be available in other languages appropriate to the local population and in braille or on tape for visually impaired service users.

☐ *Determining the level of assessment*

The Department of Health envisaged several different levels of assessment but in reality most authorities seem to have only two levels:

- A *simple assessment* follows a straight-forward request and is dealt with quickly. Examples are assessment for a bus pass or a disabled person's car badge. The assessment may well be made by a receptionist or a member of the administrative staff.
- A *comprehensive assessment*, where priority is given to those whose situation places their continued independent living in the community at risk. No one should be admitted to residential care until there has been a comprehensive assessment of their needs.

Social service authorities often have a list of criteria against which they judge whether someone should have a comprehensive assessment. It is likely that someone in Mary's situation (perhaps needing residential care or quite a lot of support at home) will meet those criteria so a comprehensive assessment will take place. The hospital social worker, Janet, has the job of arranging it.

☐ *Assessing need*

The local authority has a long (about twenty pages) assessment form, which it expects social workers or care managers to complete. Janet does not like this form as it sometimes forces her to ask inappropriate questions. On her social work training course she was taught that such assessments should not be rushed and that workers should spend time getting to know the service users, their networks and agendas. Janet feels caught between doing as she was taught, the demands of form-filling and the pressure of time.

Janet sees Mary Warwick on the ward three times, speaks to the ward nurses and interviews Mary's daughter Sarah during one of her visits to her mother. Janet also asks the district occupational therapist to visit Mary and to provide an opinion on whether she could manage at home, and if so what adaptations or equipment she might need. Janet brings all this information together in her assessment document.

After this Janet has to do a financial assessment and ask Mary about any savings and clarify the ownership of the house she lives in. This involves filling in a form with details of Mary's income and expenditure in order to work out how much she will have to pay towards services such as home care or day care. Sometimes specialist finance officers within the local authority do this. This is frequently experienced as intrusive and Mary may resent the questions or indeed refuse to give details. These 'social care' services are means-tested and so people who can afford it pay towards the cost.

☐ Care planning

Mary wants to return home and Sarah has said she will do all she can to help her mother. Mary will need quite a lot of help at home so Janet has to draw up a care plan. The local authority has defined categories of need. These are often called eligibility criteria and a typical example was given in Chapter 1. Janet's team leader agrees with Janet that Mary falls into a category where there is a high level of need. A weekly care plan is drawn up and costed. It involves an hour's home care in both the morning and the evening of each weekday. Meals on wheels will be delivered every day except Wednesday and Sunday. Attendance at a day centre is to be arranged for the Wednesday. Sarah has agreed to cover the week-end and other gaps.

It takes some weeks for this to go before by the 'panel' that allocates money. The panel is made up of senior officers of the social service authority and their task is to prioritise the competing claims as their budget is limited. In the meantime Mary remains in hospital, wanting to be at home. The medical staff and nurses understand the situation but nevertheless feel frustrated that a bed is being occupied by someone who no longer needs it.

Janet realises that Mary may now meet the criteria for the attendance allowance. This is a non-means-tested benefit for people who need some help with bodily functions. She takes the initiative and fills in the long, complicated form with Mary and Sarah. The award of this benefit will help Mary to pay for some of the charges she will have to meet. In time Mary's income will be made up of her pension, the attendance allowance, and some income support benefit (including a higher pensioner premium because attendance allowance is a qualifying criterion for this benefit).

☐ *Implementing the care plan*

When the money is finally approved, Mary is discharged and the care package is put into place. Janet has the job of ensuring that the different elements of it come together. She is on the 'purchaser' side and has to ensure that the 'providers' are arranged and in place. This means ensuring that the home care workers attend when expected, the meals are delivered and the day care arrangements have been made.

The occupational therapist has arranged for some aids to help Mary. Janet knows that the occupational therapist is also working as hard as she can to organise some adaptations to Mary's house. She is liaising with the housing department to try to obtain a disability facilities grant, which will enable some significant modifications to be made to the house, for example the installation of a stairlift or a shower. Unfortunately this is a slow process with many delays and she knows it will take many months.

☐ *Monitoring*

Janet makes sure that the people involved in the care plan have her telephone number and asks them to ring her if there are any problems. She herself monitors the situation by occasionally ringing Mary, Sarah and the home care organiser.

☐ *Review*

Monitoring can merge into review: if the situation changes in some way it will have to be reviewed. Mary manages satisfactorily for several months with the help provided, but during the winter she falls and later experiences a burglary, which distresses her greatly. She is increasingly frail and says she no longer feels she can manage living by herself. At this stage a review is necessary. Among the options to be considered would no doubt be the possibility of:

• More support being provided for Mary at home.
• Living with Sarah.
• A moving into a residential home.

All of these have significant implications and Janet has the responsibility of advising Mary on them. For example if Mary moves in with Sarah, Mary will no doubt sell her house and the proceeds of this will render her ineligible for income support benefit. She will be expected to live off this capital until it has been susbtantially reduced.

☐ *Commentary*

Community care is complicated and the care manager has to guide the service user through a system where benefits, services and housing provision intertwine. From the Department of Health guidance it is clear that the assessment of need is seen as being of central importance to the arrangements for community care and that the views of the service user should be of primary importance within these arrangements.

When it comes to working out a care plan it is important to cost it. In Mary's case, if the cost exceeds a certain amount it is likely that there will be pressure for her to enter a residential home. Janet is on the purchaser side because she is arranging the care plan. The providers include the home care service, the meal service and the day centre provision. These could be provided by the social services authority itself or by independent providers – this mixture is sometimes called the 'mixed economy of care'. The government has been especially critical of the lack of proper review of individual cases: 'Once services are being provided, they are often not reviewed' (DoH, 1998a, p. 15).

■ The background of care management

There are a variety of sources of information on the background of care management, such as the guidelines issued by the Department of Health in the early 1990s (some of which have been drawn on above), accounts of the experiences in and literature from North America, and accounts of the experience of pilot projects in the UK from the 1970s onwards.

Care management developed in North America because it was seen as a helpful way of both dealing with the fragmentation of services and containing costs. In the United States there have been over four decades of experience of care management, producing a variety of models of what care management has been and might be. Whilst there is doubt about the transferability of some of this experience to the UK because of the very real differences in social service provision, there has undoubtedly been some influence (Davies and Challis, 1986).

Care management in the UK does not have as lengthy a history as it does in North America. A number of pilot and demonstration projects were conducted in the UK during the 1970s and 1980s. These were evaluated and have influenced the development of care management. Kent Social Services experimented with care management from the late 1970s. The Thanet Community Care project was the first project in Kent and it was a collaborative venture with the Personal Services Research Unit (PSSRU) at the University of Kent. This scheme targeted a group of older people who would ordinarily have been offered residential care. As an alternative a package of care in the community was put together. The packages cost up to two-thirds of the cost of residential care. A specialist team of workers with relatively small caseloads managed the scheme. The team managed the budget themselves, which meant that they were able to use the money flexibly and modify their plans as the situation changed (Challis and Davies, 1986).

The Thanet project was followed by other pilot projects in Kent and elsewhere in the country. A scheme in Darlington aimed to provide home care to frail older people who would otherwise require long-stay hospital care. Positive results were shown in the evaluation (Challis *et al.*, 1995).

In 1983 the Department of Health and Social Security launched a 'care in the community' initiative. This involved funding 28 projects for three years. The projects were innovatory pilot schemes involving community care arrangements for people in long-stay hospitals (Renshaw, 1988). The PSSRU was given the task of promoting, monitoring and evaluating the projects.

One of the conditions of the DHSS funding of projects was that some form of care management procedure should be established for people leaving hospital. The projects showed how complicated it was to undertake the careful and sensitive transfer of vulnerable people from long-stay institutions into community settings. These projects, and the PSSRU's evaluation and monitoring of them, no doubt played some part in the care management recommendations set out in *Caring for People* (DoH, 1989a).

The introduction of care management and the form it took has to be seen in the context of the ideological programme of the Conservative government and the ideas of the New Right. Sheppard (1995, p. 56) points out that care management was influenced by the strong belief in the virtues of competition, the assumption that public management was less efficient than private management and the development of a quasi-market in social care.

Some social workers have been quite bemused by these changes and feel that the bureaucratisation, form-filling and financial assessments have brought an end to the traditional activities of social work. Certainly social work has changed, but it can be argued that it is continually evolving rather than ending (Payne, 1995). There are also some strong links to past practices, for example assessments in which the service user's views are carefully attended to are central to care management and have always been important to good practice. The next section looks at this.

■ Assessment within care management

Section 47 of the NHS&CC Act 1990 stated that, if someone appeared to be in need of community care services, then the social service authority must carry out an assessment of their needs and take this assessment into account when deciding how to meet these needs. The Department of Health described assessment as 'the cornerstone' of good quality community care (DoH, 1990) and stressed the importance of assessments being 'needs-led' (DoH, 1991b). Service users would be more involved with purchasing decisions and this would facilitate an individualised, flexible response to need (Davis *et al.*, 1997, p. 6). This was in contrast with the traditional 'service-led' assessment where practitioners were governed by the specific services their agency offered and the assessment process was dominated by whether any of these services (for example day care, home care, meals provision) would help the service user.

The reality under the 'needs-led' rhetoric has often been that practitioners have undertaken assessments under pressure, with limited resources and with very tight eligibility criteria operating. It is the difficult job of front line staff to manage these contradictions or conflicts in policy.

In the past the more qualitative approaches to assessment were seen as the essence of professional skill. Social workers, made uncertain by the changes, have often succumbed to the notion of assessment by ticking boxes. Increased power to managers and the routinisation of tasks has been the pattern in social work as in many of the public services – a process sometimes called 'neo-Taylorism' (Sheppard, 1995, p. 73). Sheppard notes that large areas of social care have experienced task routinisation and deskilling. Others have noted a deskilling and decline of social work, with assessment reduced to form filling in a fairly technical way (Hadley and Clough, 1996, p. 31). Such aspects of assessment are the very opposite of a sensitive, needs-led assessment of a person's situation. There has been and continues to be a battle as to where social work now sits on the continuum between these opposites.

In some authorities the introduction of 'information technology' has contributed to the routinisation process. Assessments which can be fed into the computer screen are obviously quick but tend to increase the practice of using impersonalised and routinised assessments. Computers have a valuable place in welfare but they should not be used to set the agenda for community care. Practitioners can fall into the trap of thinking that doing a good assessment means filling in the form correctly or inputting the information into the computer quickly and accurately.

There are clearly different ways of handling the forms. In a small-scale study Bradley *et al.* (1996, p. 38) found that 'some workers just referred to them in passing in the first interview, obtained the necessary signatures, took the occasional note and filled in the sections back at the office. Others went through stage by stage in meticulous detail with the user.' The researchers found that most social workers attempted to complete all sections of the forms, but 'The result was long tracts of mainly descriptive rather than analytic material. The net effect was to focus on the negatives rather than the strengths of an individual, immediate family or networks. This emphasis on the negatives resulted in assessors resorting to familiar responses to problems in the form of recommending standard services in their Care Plans' (ibid., p. 39).

In the debate on the nature of assessment a clear and helpful distinction is made by Smale *el al.* (1993) in a practice guide commissioned by the

Department of Health from the National Institute of Social Work. Smale *et al.* distinguish between the 'questioning model', the 'procedural model' and the 'exchange model'. Under the questioning model the assumption is that workers are experts in the problems and needs of people and that they exercise their knowledge and skill when making their assessment. They assess need, identify the resources required and take the follow-through action. The advantage of this for the agency is that it is relatively quick and straightforward. However the model focuses on the dependency needs of the individual. It tends to ignore the resources actually or potentially available in the social situation and the extent to which they could be mobilised and used.

Under the procedural model, workers operate within certain agency guidelines and criteria for the allocation of scarce resources, and they are expected to gather information as a basis for judgements. 'In this the goal of assessment is to gather information to see if the client "fits", or meets, certain criteria that will "make them eligible for services"' (ibid., p. 19). Social workers have the task of identifying those who match the need defined within the categories of service available and excluding those who do not. The agenda here is really set by the agency and those who draw up the forms within the agency.

Under the exchange model it is assumed that users, others involved and professionals all have equally valid views of the problems and can contribute to their solution. There is an exchange of information. Many people feel considerable frustration that some medical professionals assume the role of expert role on their patients, sometimes ignoring the opinions of the patients themselves. Under the exchange model it is assumed that people are experts on themselves. Smale *et al.* argue that practitioners need expertise in the process of assessment and they list four key aspects of this (Box 4.2).

Box 4.2   Aspects of expertise in assessment

- 'Expertise in facilitating people's attempts to articulate and so identify their own needs and clarify what they want.'
- 'Sensitivity to language, cultural, racial, and gender differences.'
- 'The ability to help people through major transitions involving loss.'
- 'The ability to negotiate and conciliate between people who have different perceptions, values, attitudes, expectations, wants and needs' (Smale *et al.*, 1993, p.13).

The care manager should have expertise in the process of problem solving and the ability to work towards a common understanding of the problem with all the people involved. Brown (1998) argues that the exchange model is the most appropriate approach when assessing the situation of lesbians and gay men. She argues that with this model 'the social worker has to work with individuals and systems involved within their own context, and has to "hear" what is actually being said, which is often not what we might expect to hear' (ibid., p. 110). Rather than working through a long form, finding out about what people can and cannot do and then organising care and support, the approach is instead concerned with coming to an agreement about what needs doing, when it should be done and who should do it.

Chapter 2 discussed how caring relationships and commitments are negotiated over time. Practitioners need to be conscious of these negotiations and sensitive to their historical roots (Finch and Mason, 1993). The exchange model gives particular attention to the social networks of the person. A package of care is not something that can be quickly thrown together and then left. It is usually based on fragile human relationships that may need developing and nurturing. This is skillful work. The whole of the Chapter 6 is devoted to this important issue of social networks.

It will be clear that Smale *et al.* (and this author) are critical of questioning and procedural models which are characterised by a narrow form-filling approach. Such an approach is inconsistent with any serious vision of user involvement, user empowerment and user-led services. The job of assessment requires the skills of empathy, sensitivity, information gathering, problem solving, negotiation and judgement if the service user is to be a partner in the process.

Smale *et al.* (1993) write of the ability of the worker to create a collaborative working relationship based upon the three central skills of authenticity (or congruence), empathy and respect. These are the same sort of skills that have always been associated with social work practice and were central to social work texts of thirty years ago (Truax and Carkuff, 1967). Added to the three core skills, Smale *et al.* (1993) argue that a care manager also needs to be competent in dealing with aspects of marginality, as well as in the art of challenging, conceptualising and reframing. The whole book stresses the skills and competencies needed for effective care management and assessment – skills and competencies that are very much in the mainstream of traditional social work.

Other writers also argue for this more holistic view of assessment. Morris (1997) outlines four key principles of working in partnership with people who need support in their daily lives: entitlement, the social model of disability, need-led assessment, and promoting choice and control. She writes of the links between these principles and the way in which they underpin each other: 'for example, people are entitled to expect a needs-led assessment which is based on the social model of disability and aims to promote choice and control in people's lives' (ibid., p. 2). Clifford (1998) argues for a holistic theoretical framework for all social assessments, using a critical auto/biographical methodology. He gives details of six principles that form the basis of evaluating the range of procedures from simple form-filling to complex multi-disciplinary assessments.

The role of social workers in financial assessments also needs to be considered. Such assessments are usually concerned with seeing how much the service users should contribute towards the cost of the services provided. However they should also be used to ensure that service users receive all the benefits that are available to them. Financial assessment procedures vary between local authorities. This area has often been a new and testing one for social workers working with adults in the community. Questions have to be asked about income, pensions, benefits claimed, insurance policies, income tax allowances, capital/savings, extra expenses incurred as a result of disability or illness, and other outgoings (Mares, 1996). Mares argues that workers should make the most productive use of this financial assessment process and not regard it simply as an administrative chore. The worker needs to be well informed and then to use the opportunity 'to explore users' and carers' financial situation and possible sources of financial support, to give them clear information about their rights, and, where appropriate, to tell them about independent sources of advice' (ibid., p. 132).

In an interesting study on the dilemmas of financial assessment, Bradley and Manthorpe (1997) use three case studies to draw out the complexities of finance and the way in which finance impinges directly on aspects of assessment and care plans.

■ The experience of care management and assessment

The community care changes raised questions about who was to be assessed and how 'need' was to be defined. If needs were defined widely and generously, then there were large resource and personnel implications. How do you 'square the circle', as Ellis (1993) put it. Lewis and Glennerster (1996) argue that the circle was squared by the Chief Inspector of Social Services in December 1992, who argued that:

- Authorities do not have a duty to assess on request, but only when they think that the person may be in need of services they provide.
- The assessment of need and the decision about which services should be provided are separate stages in the process (CI(92)34; DoH, 1992).

According to Lewis and Glennerster (1996, p. 15), 'In short, a judgment of need can be made before an assessment of need and even though a person may be judged in need the legislation does not require action to meet it. Any apprentices in circle squaring should take careful note. This is a masterpiece of the art form'.

At the end of 1993 the Audit Commission warned local authorities of the importance of establishing firm eligibility criteria for services such that there would be ' just enough people with needs to exactly use up their budget (or be prepared to adjust their budgets)' (Audit Commission, 1993, para. 15).

It is in these ways (and those outlined in Chapter 1) that local authorities have managed some of the contradictions, resulting in a wide variety of types of care management and methods of assessment. The contradictions trickle down to front line workers, who have to try to find a way through them. There are a range of different pressures on and expectations of care managers, some of which are listed in Box 4.3.

Box 4.3   Differing expectations and pressures on care managers

- Implementing anti-oppressive practices (Thompson, 1997).
- Empowering service users.
- Working within limited resources and therefore rationing.
- Carrying out 'needs-led' assessments.
- Conducting financial assessments.
- Working in an interprofessional way.
- Encouraging greater involvement of users and carers.
- Working within a system that gives more powers to managers and routinises tasks.

In this complicated area it falls to the front line practitioner to deal with all the contradictions. As in other areas of the public services it is the 'street level' worker (Lipsky, 1980) who has to find a way through these contradictions and confront an array of policies with conflicting aims. It needs to be clearly appreciated that not all these expectations can be met and that if workers are to find a way through the contradictions they have to evolve 'survival techniques'.

One way of working within the contradictions is for care managers to paint a gloomier picture of the service user than is actually the case in order to meet a certain criterion. When this happens there is a built-in push towards pathology rather than empowerment. Here the assessment 'trick' is to portray the potential service in as 'deserving' a light as possible – according to the particular eligibility or assessment criteria. The practitioner's concern is to write down on the assessment form what people cannot do in order to achieve some sort of service for them. It can be extremely frustrating to do a full assessment and then to be told that the situation falls outside the eligibility criteria for services to be made available. The alternative is for the practitioner to use the eligibility criteria to block the possibility of a service before the full assessment is done (Davis *et al.*, 1997, p. 49). Decisions are made to resolve the real tension between needs and resources by targeting (Lewis and Glennerster, 1996 p. 163). Only those considered to be most at risk receive an assessment (ibid.).

In reality, when resources are short 'needs-led' assessment turns into 'risk-based' assessment. Davis *et al.* (1997) note how the changes provide little scope for the practitioner to engage in empowering assessment practice. The new 'assessment arrangements reflect a medical model of disability.

Eligibility criteria based on measures of risk and dependency encourage assessors to see need in terms of individual impairment rather than socially created discrimination, there is a marked tension here between professional values and agency agendas' (ibid., p. 16).

Reports on the introduction of care management have described the experience of front line workers as stressful (Hadley and Clough, 1996; Lewis and Glennerster, 1996). In a study of fifteen people involved in the changes Hadley and Clough paint a bleak picture, as indicated by the title of their work – *Care in Chaos*. They talk of the 'massive scale' of the changes. These changes were not extensively piloted and Hadley and Clough (1996, p. 17) consider that, 'The proposals were in these ways revolutionary not evolutionary, and the belief that they would work would seem to have owed more to ideology than reason'.

In their study of assessment in relation to disabled people and their carers, Davis *et al.* (1997) explored the effects of the new assessment regulations in two social services authorities. They interviewed 50 disabled people and 23 carers, and observed how practitioners in six social work teams were making their assessment decisions. They found that both authorities had a standardised approach to assessment as set out in operational guidelines. Decisions about access to assessment were influenced by risk-based service criteria linked to budget considerations. Teams operated differently in determining assessment eligibility and the process of assessment was also dealt with differently by the teams.

Against the thrust of policy and operational guidance, the researchers found that the six teams could be grouped into three types in relation to assessment and that there was a wide variation between these three groupings. People's access to and experience of assessment varied considerably according to the type of team conducting the assessment. The differences seemed to reflect both the organisational function of the teams and the coping mechanisms of front line staff under differing organisational demands and pressures.

Some idea of the contrast in the assessment procedures is reflected in the following quotation:

> Disabled people and carers in this study accessed assessment through a range of social work contacts. Some were assessed without seeing or speaking to a social worker. Some had only telephone contacts; others brief face-to-face contacts; some had lengthy or repeated contact. Whatever the type of contact, few people understood that an investigation of their needs was being undertaken (Davis *et al.*, 1997, p. 58).

Not only is the contrast between the assessments described in this study interesting, so too is the contrast between many of these assessments and the Department of Health's guidelines on assessment in care management (DoH, 1991b).

For most of the disabled people in Davis *et al.*'s study 'assessment' meant little. Assessment as a process that takes account of the wishes of those being assessed and where possible includes their active participation did not feature in the accounts most people gave of their contact with social workers. Davis *et al.* write that 'most people were not aware that they had a right to assessment or that their needs had been considered by a social worker' (ibid., p. 52). The authors note that people's lack of awareness of being a part, active or otherwise, of an assessment process was similar to the findings of other studies that have sought disabled people's and carers' views of community care services. Baldock and Ungerson (1994), for example, researched the assessment experiences of 32 stroke victims and found that they had little awareness of when or how an assessment had taken place.

Davis *et al.* state that much of the practice they observed was based on the procedural model of Smale *et al.* (1993). As outlined above, the goal of assessment under this model is to determine whether the service user meets a set of eligibility criteria. When these criteria are defined, services are effectively preallocated for generally identified needs. Social workers must then decide who matches what level of need, as defined within the categories of service available, and exclude those deemed ineligible. The requirements of form-filling and providing data for computers encouraged this model.

Most of the disabled people and carers in Davis *et al.*'s study understood little about the purpose of the assessment procedures in which they found themselves. Yet it was well understood and highly rated when the procedure was informed by a commitment to partnership. In this study the specialist teams were more likely to carry out assessments in a collaborative way with service users.

The researchers concluded that most of the assessments ignored the opportunity to build on strategies that disabled people and their carers had created for themselves. Much assessment was experienced as a barrier rather than a helpful way of maximising choice and independence. Some of the problems from the disabled person's point of view are summarised in Box 4.4 (Davis *et al.*, 1997).

Box 4.4   *Problems with assessment*

- Practioners did not leave a name and contact number.
- With regard to paperwork, 'concern with completing items on checklists and forms blunted responsiveness to what disabled people and carers were saying and discouraged disabled people and carers from sharing more information about their situations' (ibid., p. 58).
- Practitioners used jargon.
- There were greater problems for those whose first language was not English.
- There were long delays in social services' responses.
- There was a strict division between service users and carers – which does not match reality.

In summary, the authors consider that 'Accessing assessment, from the viewpoint of most of the disabled people and carers interviewed, was an experience of uncertainty, confusion, marginalisation and exclusion' (ibid. p. 71). They pose the question as to whether this assessment practice can change.

Another study that revealed great dissatisfaction with the process of assessment was Priestley's (1999) study of disabled people in Derbyshire, where there were 'delays, lack of information, poor communication, patronising attitudes, and the absence of collaborative working' (ibid., p. 94). Some disabled people and writers have argued in favour of self-assessment followed by self-management (ibid.). Care management resulting from the NHS&CC Act 1990 is generally dominated by professional practitioners, but direct payment schemes are a move in the direction of self-assessment and management. However, it can be a big jump from being dependent on whatever services are provided by others to managing your own services, and so careful transitional planning and support may be needed. For example people may well need help with recruitment, interviewing and employment relations (ibid.). These ideas of self-management and independent living will be returned to in Chapter 7.

■ Practice issues

One lesson to be gained from this chapter is that there are many varieties of care management and assessment, so if practitioners feel very frustrated by what exists locally they can press for change and better practice – perhaps along the lines of the 'exchange' model outlined above.

The latter part of the chapter looked at a number of issues relating to the practice of assessment and care management. It is clear that there are many contradictions in the work, as shown in Box 4.2, and it is hard for practitioners to find a way through the conflicting expectations. The issue of empowerment will be explored more fully in Chapter 7, but it is important to acknowledge the very real contradictions in policy that exist and have to be resolved by practitioners. Understanding what 'survival techniques' are being used allows questions to be asked about whether they are the best ones. 'Survival techniques' that are at the expense of the service user should be questioned.

Practioners need to be fully aware of the procedures used in their area in relation to assessment, care management, eligibility criteria and direct payments. Service users are entitled to know how to challenge decisions and various options are open to them, each with advantages and disadvantages. Under the NHS&CC Act 1990 all social service authorities most have a complaints procedure. There is also an NHS complaints procedure. Users can contact the health service or local authority ombudsman. Grievances can be made known to local representatives such as councillors and MPs, or directly to the government. A number of community care grievances have gone through the courts to a judicial review, which is the main ground of legal challenge to local authorities (Mandelstam, 1999).

Care management has largely been organised within social service authorities and social service staff have usually taken the leading role. Care managers must be sensitive to the needs of carers (see Chapter 2) and the 'interweaving' of formal and informal modes of care is crucial. Care managers also need to work in partnership with other agencies involved in community care (as outlined in Chapter 3). This issue of 'inter-professional working' is the subject of the following chapter.

☐ *Further reading*

P. Mares, *Business Skills for Care Management* (London: Age Concern, 1996). This book introduces in a clear way some of the 'business skills' that may be helpful in the care management role. This includes handling contracts, costing care packages, negotiating prices with providers and monitoring the quality of service.

J. Morris, *Community Care: Working in Partnership with Service Users* (Birmingham: Venture Press, 1997). In this book Morris outlines four key principles for working in partnership with people who need support in their daily lives: entitlement, the social model of disability, needs-led assessment, and promoting choice and control. It is a 'practitioner's guide' that might be hard to live up to but is worth aspiring to.

☐ *World Wide Web site*

In research volume 3, chapter 5, of the Royal Commission on Long Term Care there is an overview of studies on care management during the 1990s. This can be accessed at

http://www.open.gov.uk/royal-commission-elderly/

Within the 'Final Report' you need to scroll down to Appendix 8 in order to access the research volumes.

■ *Chapter 5* ■

Interprofessional Issues in Community Care

Chapter summary
This chapter: • Describes the background to and causes of poor interprofessional working.   • Discusses attempts and initiatives to improve interprofessional working.   • Provides an example of interprofessional working in the mental health field in relation to the care programme approach and care management by community mental health teams.

■ Introduction

Effective collaboration between agencies is a central issue in all aspects of community care not just in relation to older people and disabled people but also in areas such as adult abuse, palliative care, drug and alcohol abuse, and domestic violence. Areas of work that should involve interprofessional collaboration include assessment of need, discharge from hospital, care management systems and working across the developing mixed economy of welfare (Leathard, 1994, p. 14).

Loxley (1997, p. 90) argues that interprofessional collaboration is 'a device for managing and organising resources, and a technique for delivering services. To succeed practitioners, managers and policy makers require sufficient knowledge, a repertoire of relevant skills, appropriate structures for the exchange of information and resources, and processes which facilitate relationships. No one of these alone is sufficient; all are necessary.'

There are a range of general factors behind poor interprofessional working, as shown in Box 5.1.

Box 5.1   Factors behind poor interprofessional working
• A large number of organisations may be involved in providing a variety of different caring and accommodation services.   • These organisations have different structures, which makes communication at various levels difficult.

- Different organisations have different budgets and financial arrangements.
- Some of the organisations have different geographical boundaries.
- There has been weak legislative and policy guidance on interprofessional working.
- Workers within organisations have different backgrounds, remuneration, occupational training, culture and language, which contribute to professional barriers, mistrust, misunderstanding and disagreements.

Some writers have used the idea of 'tribes' to emphasise the differences and the problems. Dalley (1989, p. 116), for example, writes of 'tribal allegiances' which are 'not necessarily grounded in genuine differences of view but are, rather, the product of unfounded and stereotypical assumptions about those located outside the inclusive boundaries of organisations and culture'.

Some aspects of the 1990s community care changes have made the situation more difficult. Firstly, the changing boundaries described in Chapter 3 led to increased tension between agencies. Secondly, the community care changes brought in competition and deliberately created 'markets'. If groups and agencies are competing in a market situation then this may work against the trust needed to share information and resources and create good, effective cooperation. Cooperation is in tension with the ethos of competition. The concept of the purchaser/provider split has not assisted collaboration and may actively operate against it. Whilst collaboration might be easier at the purchasing (or commissioning) level, it is more difficult at the provider level, where organisations and agencies may be in competition with one another (Lewis and Glennerster, 1996).

■ Background to the problems

In order to understand how the major differences between services have developed, it is necessary to go back to the setting up of the postwar welfare state. In the postwar settlement community services were shared between various authorities. As a result of the reorganisation of both the health service and personal social services in the early 1970s the occupational therapy service, the home help service and the social work service came under the jurisdiction of social service authorities, while the community nursing service became part of the health service. So for example, community nursing and home care which had previously been part of the same local authority structure, now were in very separate structures. These structural barriers between service providers were superimposed on the professional barriers. By the mid 1970s social work was the realm of local government whilst medicine and nursing were outside local government. These different structures and different types of accountability meant that barriers and divisions were created between the local authorities, the community nursing services, the hospital services and general practitioners.

Since then there have been a number of attempts to bring about better collaboration. Examples of this in the 1970s and 1980s were joint planning and joint financing. In England and Wales joint consultative committees and joint care planning teams were established to try to achieve better cooperation. Joint financing was also introduced with the aim of stimulating and encouraging joint working. Scotland had liaison committees on a voluntary basis.

However the effectiveness of these initiatives, which were the main vehicle for promoting collaboration, was very limited. Commentators and researchers largely agree that joint planning and joint financing by the health and local authorities during the 1970s and 1980s were weak and ineffective (Wistow and Brooks, 1988; Stockford, 1988; Lewis and Glennerster, 1996).

Given this experience, the exhortation in the 1990s for a 'seamless service' without dramatic changes seemed unrealistic. The Audit Commission (1986) was in no doubt that the situation was poor in respect of service integration and coordination. Reorganisation was needed and the commission recommended that:

- Local authorities should be responsible for mentally and physically handicapped people in the community.
- The lead authority for mentally ill people should be the National Health Service.
- For older people a single budget should be created in each area. There should be a single manager, with funds being provided by the local authority and the National Health Service.

These radical suggestions were not taken up in the Griffiths Report (1988) or *Caring for People* (DoH, 1989a), both of which recommended that the structures remain the same. Thus in relation to interprofessional working there was no reorganisation of agencies but there was a call for improved coordination. Social service authorities were put in overall charge of community care and hopes were pinned on care management as a means of achieving better integration.

The exception to the above is Northern Ireland. As noted in Chapter 1, Northern Ireland has combined services under four ministerially appointed Health and Social Services Boards, set up in 1973 and responsible for both health and social services. The House of Commons Health Committee has looked to the integrated service of Northern Ireland as a possible model for the rest of the UK arguing that 'we found much to admire in the integrated model adopted in Northern Ireland' (HoC, 1999, para. 68).

In the absence of structural reorganisation of structures another way forward in the early 1990s would have been to have established strong financial inducements and a powerful legal mandate. Some efforts were made in this direction but they were limited. In 1993 the payment of the Sspecial Transitional Grant was made conditional on health authorities and social service authorities establishing local agreements on the placement of people in nursing home beds and on hospital discharge arrangements. On the legal side, Section 46 of the NHS&CC Act 1990 required local authorities to consult a range of organisations when formulating and reviewing community care plans. The Act also imposed a duty on social service authorities to notify the local housing authority and appropriate health services and invite them to assist in assessment when a potential housing or health need was identified. However no obligation was imposed on the housing authorities or the health services actually to give assistance. This legal mandate clearly could have been stronger. The community care changes of the early 1990s did not address the reorganisation of services or impose a powerful legal mandate. As before, the need remained to make structures work effectively and efficiently together so that users had the best possible service and funders the best possible value for money.

Government policy has often assumed that there are clearcut distinctions between health and social care. There are differences, but there are also considerable areas of overlap, making attempts at clear distinctions rather futile. One source of friction between professionals is the ambiguity about who is responsible for what. There is some interesting material on this issue in the Department of Health's guide to care management (DoH, 1991a). What is especially interesting is that the guide itself indicates large areas of needs that may fall under either health care or social care.

Chapter 3 noted that the strategy in the early 1990s seemed to be to demedicalise provision and define many activities as social care rather than medical care. Hence there was a cost-shunting from the free health services to the means-tested social services, which provided the potential for increased tension between workers in the health and social care sectors. Chapter 3 indicated that the health authorities redefined their areas of responsibility for continuing care to such an extent that an alarmed government took steps to prevent it from going any further. At the point of the interface between workers at the bottom of their organisational hierarchy it was not surprising that it was hard to make interprofessional practice work. What was surprising was that workers often did overcome many of the structural problems, frequently because of their commitment to a public service ethos.

In their study of the implementation of the 1990 community care legislation by five local authorities, Lewis and Glennerster (1996, p. 167) state that 'action to achieve collaboration in community care has taken a variety of forms in the 1990s. Authorities were faced with the question of what to do about the elaborate 1980s joint planning machinery.' Lewis and Glennerster argue that it was not abolished but 'reworked in relation to the emergence of the purchaser-provider splits and renamed "joint commissioning"' (ibid., p. 167). Joint commissioning was defined as 'the process in which two or more commissioning agencies act together to coordinate their commissioning, taking joint responsibility for translating strategy into action' (DoH, 1995b, p. 2). Whilst the district health authorities and social service authorities were central players in joint commissioning, housing departments, family health service authorities, GPs, GP fundholders and other providers of health and social care could also be involved. Joint commissioning was seen as a more productive way forward than joint planning and joint financing. Old structures of joint planning still existed but had been modified and revamped in the 1990s (Lewis and Glennerster, 1996).

Joint commissioning was seen as a way of collectively taking community care forward after the failure of joint planning (Poxton, 1996; Leathard, 1997). According to Poxton (1996, p. 143),

> In essence, joint commissioning seeks to bring together some or all of the commissioning functions of a number of different agencies, usually with health and social services at the core. It may be focused on a particular user group, on a range of services, on a geographical locality, or even on the needs of a particular individual.

Lewis and Glennerster (1996, p. 168) argue that many of the local authorities they studied

> began with the idea that they would eventually either make purchasing decisions in conjunction with health authorities or actually engage in joint purchasing. It is not evident that joint commissioning in this sense is in sight, but what seems to have happened, paradoxically, is that the new joint commissioning structures have provided a more effective means of joint planning.

They also argue that there was a move by all five authorities in their study towards what they called 'compatible commissioning' – collaboration involving 'agreement on the framework within which purchasers from the statutory authorities will purchase' (ibid., p. 184). Hence their view that structures have emerged that increase the possibility of effective joint planning. However their bleak assessment is that without drastic action 'The fundamental conflicts between agencies that are financed separately, administered separately, staffed by different professions and run within different statutory frameworks are so great that no joint commissioning or joint planning has much hope of succeeding' (ibid., p. 186).

■ The Labour government and the 'Berlin Wall'

The achievement of better inter-agency working was a priority for the Labour government after its election in 1997. It stressed this in a variety of documents, initiatives and proposals, for example 'The Government has made it one of its top priorities since coming to office to bring down the "Berlin Wall" that can divide health and social services, and to create a system of integrated care that puts users at the centre of service provision' (DoH, 1998a, para. 6.5). There were no proposals for major structural change in the sense of integrating services within one organisation. 'Major structural change is not the answer' (DoH, 1998c, p. 5). Rather the government's policy was to move towards pooled budgets, lead commissioning and integrated provision through enactment of the necessary legislation.

The overall strategy is made up of a number of key elements. Firstly, Health Improvement Programmes (HImPs) provide the overall strategic context. These are local strategies for improving health and health care and delivering better integrated care. There is a partnership component to them. HImPs must be agreed by partner agencies, after consultation with relevant bodies such as those in the voluntary sector. They are seen as the vehicle for developing a shared local response to national priorities and targets, as well as priorities for action in response to local needs. Different groups are involved in shaping the programmes, although they are led by the health authority. Secondly, there is a new duty of partnership on all bodies in the NHS and the local authority to work together to promote the well-being of the local community. Local authority chief executives participate in health authority meetings. Thirdly, all legislative constraints on the pooling of money, lead commissioning and integrated provision have been removed (DoH, 1998d). Fourthly, the Primary Care Groups/Trusts and their counterparts in Scotland, Wales and Northern Ireland include a representative of social service authorities and are expected to work effectively with local authority bodies. Fifthly, the health service and local authorities were asked to draw up Joint Investment Plans (JIPs), based on joint assessments of need and shared objectives for vulnerable groups. These were in place in 1999 and initially concentrated on services for older people.

There are other initiatives that the government hopes will help to chip away at the Berlin Wall. Some of the main ones are described in Box 5.2.

Box 5.2   Initiatives involving inter-agency working

In 1998 the government introduced 11 pilot zones to test new collaborative models of care. A further 15 were added later. They all started during 1999. These 'health action zones' have the backing of a consortium of local agencies and a five-year 'outcome-based' plan. A key aim is to break down the barriers between health and social services and between professionals, particularly in areas of high deprivation. Means of bringing this about are the joint management of health and social services budgets and networks of one-stop primary care centres.

An initiative entitled 'Better Services for Vulnerable People' was launched in October 1997 in England. This required all health and local authorities to draw up Joint Investment Plans for services that would help people obtain the care they needed while avoiding unnecessary hospital or care home admissions. These services would typically include specialist rehabilitation services and hospital discharge teams.

The national programme, 'Better Government for Older People', led by the Cabinet Office, set up 28 local pilot schemes across the UK to develop and test integrated inter-agency strategies on the ground, and examine innovative ways of delivering services in a coordinated and user-friendly way.

Other initiatives such as the Long-term Care Charter and the development of National Service Frameworks all required inter-agency working (DoH, 1998a).

In a discussion document entitled 'Partnership in Action' (DoH, 1998d) the government stressed yet again that disputes and arguments about health and social care boundaries were unacceptable. Emphasis would be given to pooling health and social care budgets and the joint commissioning of services.

■ Mental health as an illustration of issues in interprofessional working

It was mentioned at the start of this chapter that interprofessional working is an important aspect of every area of community care. In order to analyse this issue we shall look at mental health provision. This area has sometimes resembled a battleground between health and social care, and a number of reports have indicated that poor inter-agency working is a real problem in the mental health services (Audit Commission, 1994; Ritchie *et al*, 1994; Utting, 1994). In addition to the problems outlined earlier in the chapter, there is also the historical domination by psychiatrists, often leading to tensions over leadership and control.

It has been noted how over the past thirty years there has been a gradual but substantial change from hospital-based to community-based mental health services. The management of these services has caused considerable problems and there has been mounting public criticism of the policy. A strong media campaign has repeatedly asserted that community care has failed in the case of mental health service users. There have been a number of inquiries resulting in policy changes – principally the development of the care programme approach (CPA), the further development of community mental health teams (CMHTs), supervision registers and supervised discharge.

People with mental health problems have a diversity of needs that span a variety of agencies and workers. These agencies have different structures, managements and cultures. Professional workers are trained on different courses, often in different institutions. There has been relatively little joint training. The segregation of professional training and job structures allows stereotypes of workers in groups to develop. These divisions can impede the delivery of effective service. This section looks first at CPAs and care management, both of which are concerned with improving interprofessional working, and then at the work of CMHTs.

■ The care programme approach and care management

During the 1960s and 1970s there were a number of inquiries into hospital scandals, usually involving patients being badly treated by abusive staff in an abusive care regime. During the 1980s and especially the 1990s further inquiries often raised profound anxiety about the policy and practice of community care. In 1988 came *The Report of the Committee of Inquiry into the Care and Aftercare of Miss Sharon Campbell*, who had knifed to death her former social worker, Isabel Schwarz, at Bexley Hospital. The Campbell inquiry's recommendations led to the CPA (Spokes *et al.*, 1988).

One of the main reasons for introducing the CPA was to try to improve interprofessional communication and coordination. Interprofessional work was viewed as central to achieving a better service and the CPA was seen as a means of bringing this about. Health authorities are required to develop a CPA for people with a severe mental illness (people referred to specialist psychiatric services). The approach requires district health authorities, in collaboration with social service authorities, to design and implement arrangements for treating service users in the community and ensuring that they receive the necessary care. Under CPA the needs of each patient, in relation both to continuing health care and to social care, are assessed before discharge. Each patient has a key worker whose task it is to keep in touch with the patient in the community. The essential elements of the CPA are shown in Box 5.3.

Box 5.3   The four main elements of the care programme approach

- 'systematic arrangements for assessing the health and social needs of people accepted by the specialist psychiatric services;
- the formulation of a care plan which addresses the identified health and social care needs;
- the appointment of a key worker to keep in close touch with the patient and monitor care;
- regular review, and if need be, agreed changes in the care plan' (DoH, 1995a, p. 14).

The interprofessional aspect of CPA is illustrated by the following extract:

Specialist psychiatric services are provided by a multi-disciplinary team of individuals each with his or her particular skills and experience. It is this dimension that makes inter-agency working so crucial, particularly for severely mentally ill people. The multi-disciplinary CPA can only function where all those in the team work effectively together, for the good of the patient (DoH, 1995a, p. 14).

The CPA was slow to be implemented. A 'tiered' approach was suggested. This involved a minimal CPA for individuals who had low support needs that were likely to remain stable; a more complex CPA for those who needed support from more than one type of service and whose needs were less likely to remain stable; and a full, multidisciplinary CPA for individuals suffering from severe social dysfunction, whose needs were likely to be highly volatile, or who represented a significant risk (DoH, 1995a).

One of the strangest policy developments in community care was the simultaneous introduction of two separate but similar systems of caring for people with mental health problems, namely the care management and the care programme approach. Care management and CPA are similar in that they both include the same core tasks of assessment, planning, implementation and review. They are different in that CPA includes a key worker idea (providing direct support and counselling) in contrast to a care manager, who organises and coordinates support. They are also different in that CPA is health-led and care management is local authority-led (DoH, 1990). Reports during the 1990s indicated that there was continuous confusion about these different procedures (North *et al.*, 1993; Audit Commission, 1994; DoH, 1994).

In 1996 the Department of Health issued a publication entitled *Building Bridges*, which was a guide to arrangements for interagency work in the care and protection of severely mentally ill people (DoH, 1995a). It outlined the roles of agencies involved in caring for mentally ill people and stressed that 'The CPA is the cornerstone of the Government's mental health policy' (ibid., p. 45). The Department of Health provided no rationale for having two similar case planning approaches with different titles, simply arguing that, 'If properly implemented, multi-disciplinary assessment will ensure that the duty to make a community care assessment is fully discharged as part of the CPA, and there should not be a need for separate assessments' (ibid., p. 15). It was argued that the two systems could be integrated by treating the CPA as a specialist variant of care management for people with mental health problems (ibid., p. 56). After its election in 1997 the Labour government continued to stress the importance of care management and CPA for the delivery of effective treatment and care (DoH, 1998c).

☐ *Case study — Christopher Clunis*

Building Bridges (DoH, 1995a), referred to above, was produced in response to the Ritchie Report on the murder of Jonathan Zito by Christopher Clunis (Ritchie *et al.*, 1994). This was probably the best known mental health inquiry report of the 1990s and it filled 130 pages with 78 detailed recommendations. Recurring themes in the report were the missed opportunities and failure of communication. For example:

- A large number of psychiatrists and social workers had been temporarily responsible for Clunis's care over six years. At one time he had asked to see a psychiatrist in order to review the medication he was on, but he had not been seen for thirteen months.
- A GP whom Clunis had visited had struck him off his list because he was abusive and threatening.
- Over several years there had been a number of warning signs of Clunis's tendency for violence, including the use of knives in some potentially fatal incidents before the actual incident with Jonathan Zito. For example Clunis had stabbed a fellow hostel inmate and had been charged with causing grievous bodily harm with intent. The police had made little effort to trace the victim before the case came to court and no effort to obtain independent evidence. The case was dropped.
- A number of agencies had failed to pass on information about Clunis's acts of violence.
- There had been both ambiguous definition and ambiguous allocation of responsibilities within the mental health services.
- The various agencies involved had not attempted to involve Clunis's family in his care, despite the fact that his sister in particular had been in reasonably regular contact with him.

The Ritchie Report concluded that Clunis' care was 'a catalogue of failure and missed opportunity' (ibid., p. 105) from 1987 until 1992. Over this period Clunis had stayed in various psychiatric units and hostels for the homeless, unable to care for himself because of his mental illness. At various points there had been both the opportunity and the legal power to do something, but nothing had been done. Clunis had repeatedly fallen through the nets of care, with overstretched agencies apparently having neither the will nor the determination to work together in his interests. It was clear that there should have been better communication and coordination between agencies and a better working partnership with Clunis's family.

Another clear theme of the report was that the problem could not be blamed on a lack of resources. In his introduction to *Building Bridges* (part of the government's response to the Ritchie Report) the Parliamentary Under Secretary stated that:

> People who are severely mentally ill are likely to be receiving health and social care from a number of different agencies in the statutory, voluntary and independent sectors. All those involved need to work closely

together to ensure that their combined resources are used to best effect and, most importantly, that vulnerable patients do not fall victim to gaps in service provision. Links between health and social services are of course vital, but they are by no means the only ones which need to be made (DoH, 1995a).

Building Bridges highlighted the need for better sharing of relevant information and for a better coordination of services: 'The key principle underlying good community care for mentally ill people is that caring for this client group is not the job of one agency alone, just as it is not the responsibility of one professional group alone' (ibid., p. 26). Whilst it recognised that service providers were increasingly working in teams, the Department of Health's recommendations and subsequent government guidelines left unresolved important questions of accountability and responsibility among practitioners working in multidisciplinary teams. These ambiguities are long-standing and contribute to ambivalence about multidisciplinary teams among professional practitioners (Galvin and McCarthy, 1994). The next section looks at this in more detail.

□ Community Mental Health Teams

According to Wells, 'Community Mental Health Teams (CMHT) have been identified as the vehicle through which mental health care in the community, encapsulated in the "Care Programme Approach" should be delivered' (Wells, 1997, p. 333). Two mechanisms (CPAs and CMHTs) are in place to help make multidisciplinary working effective within the mental health field. *Building Bridges* also stressed the importance of teams: 'Specialist services working in hospitals and the community are increasingly working in teams. This is recognised as the most effective way of delivering multi-disciplinary, flexible services which the principles outlined above demand' (DoH, 1995a, p. 35).

That CMHTs were viewed as central to community mental health care was reinforced by the Department of Health in its publication *Spectrum of Care* (1996), 'CMHTs cover a defined population group. This means each team is responsible for delivering and coordinating a specialised level of care. The teams include: social workers; mental health nurses; psychologists; occupational therapists; and psychiatrists' (p. 5).

There is no agreement on exactly what constitutes a CMHT. In a study of CMHTs conducted by the Sainsbury Centre they were defined as 'a team of four or more members, from two or more disciplines, that is recognised as a CMHT by service managers, services adults with mental health problems as its identified client group, does most of its work outside hospitals (although it may be hospital-based) and offers a wider range of services than simply structured day care' (Onyett *et al.*, 1995, p. 3). Onyett *et al.* identified 517 CMHTs in 144 health authorities in England.

They obtained details from 302 (58 per cent) of these and found varied structures, settings and skill mixes. In terms of CMHT composition, most numerous were community psychiatric nurses (in 93 per cent of teams), social workers (86 per cent) and administrative staff (85 per cent), followed by consultant psychiatrists (79 per cent), clinical psychologists (72 per cent) and occupational therapists (69 per cent).

A frequent criticism of CMHTs is that the role of team members is not clear. Being members of two groups – a professional discipline and an interdisciplinary team – they can be torn in two directions. Onyett *et al.* suggest that

> It might therefore be predicted that the ideal conditions for team membership would be where a positive sense of belonging to the team can exist alongside continued professional identification. This is most likely to occur when the discipline has a clear and valued role within the team, which in turn requires that the team itself has a clear role (ibid., p. 22).

An interesting debate has emerged as to whether CMHTs can overcome all the problems and actually bring about effective multidisciplinary working practices. Perhaps the strongest argument against their ability to do this has come from Galvin and McCarthy (1994), who argue that they are 'fatally flawed' and that the provision they offer is unfocused, inefficient and of poor quality. They argue that this is an inadequate model and that alternative models of mental health service provision are needed. A main cause of the problem is the complexity of the tasks the teams have to tackle which they are poorly equipped to handle. Too much has been expected of them.

Galvin and McCarthy argue that the CMHTs have an overambitious agenda; that the need for CMHTs is assumed rather than argued for; that issues of accountability and responsibility are fudged both within the CMHT and in relation to external management. Teams are left to cope with problems that are beyond them – differences of history, policy, mechanism and goals. 'Teams are expected to resolve complex national issues such as the status of individual members, professional training, levels of competence, legal status, entitlement to practice autonomously, and the functional interrelationships between professional groups without any definitive central policies or even guidance' (ibid., p. 164). These issues are far too significant and distant to be resolved by improving the processes locally within the teams. CMHTs appear as though they are tackling the community mental health agenda but they are not. 'CMHTs are attractive because they provide a convenient means of pushing conflicts down the system' (ibid., p. 165). Galvin and McCarthy stress the importance of not dodging issues that arise higher up the system.

The views propounded by Galvin and McCarthy are just one perspective on the issue and they are at one end of a continuum. The consensus however is very much in favour of CMHTs as a key means of delivering community mental health care. Onyett and Ford (1996), for example, do not accept that the concept of multidisciplinary teamworking is inherently flawed and they make a convincing case for its continuation.

Onyett argues that CMHTs, far from being a failed project, are a key vehicle for collaborative care but that attention needs to be given to questions of implementation (Onyett, 1997). He notes that the development of case management was a US social policy measure to improve targeting, followed in the UK by CPA and care management. He argues that there were disappointing outcomes in case management and keyworking when they operated as a means of service coordination and follow-up outside a multidisciplinary team (ibid., p. 264). Thus CPAs need CMHTs in order to work effectively.

In the United States, research indicates that community mental health teams and centres failed to prioritise services for people with severe and long-term mental health problems until there was a switch to an emphasis on case management coordination (Onyett *et al.*, 1994). Similarly in the UK, CMHTs have been criticised for neglecting people with severe mental heath problems (Patmore and Weaver, 1991), and case management coordination (CPA and care management) has been developed to help address this issue.

Guidance on CPA and care management has stressed the importance of the multidisciplinary team working for people with severe, long-term mental health problems. The main vehicle for multidisciplinary team working is the CMHT and thus it has been proposed that CPA and care management be integrated within CMHTs. Other important elements for effective interprofessional working are a joint strategy, good information sharing, joint training and management support for a culture of inter-professional communication (Hancock and Villeneau, 1997, p. 33).

The Department of Health stresses that people with mental health problems need help from a range of services and that these are frequently fractured and disjointed (DoH, 1998c). It agrees that there is a lack of clarity about who is responsible for what, and argues that 'An effective NHS and social care mental health service is comprised of a series of components which to work well, need to work together' (ibid., para. 4.56). Practitioners should continue their work within CMHTs but with greater emphasis on the provision of crisis services and assertive outreach.

■ Practice issues

On the ground it can often feel as though there is a great deal of personal conflict between different professional workers, but this is usually symptomatic of underlying structural and organisational problems. It is important for practitioners to keep this in mind. It is too easy to fall into the trap of blaming the woman/man in the agency around the corner for things that are going wrong rather than understanding and appreciating the wider context.

The reasons for the difficulties are many and complex so there are no easy solutions. There is a need for changes at all levels – political, organisational, managerial and educational. However this should not be an excuse for practitioners to do nothing. It is worth reflecting on the following quotation from the Brazilian educationalist Paulo Freire: 'How can I enter dialogue if I always project ignorance on to others and never perceive my own?' (Freire, 1972, p. 63).

A variety of initiatives can be taken at the personal and local level. Freire's comment suggests the value of finding out about the work and values of other workers. It is all too easy to become embroiled in one's own speciality and lose one's sense of a shared aim. Just as GPs and community nurses are not experts on social care, neither are social workers experts on health and medical care. There is a need for mutual respect, and for listening to and learning from others' experiences and expertise.

Interprofessional working is increasingly taking place in teams. This chapter has discussed some of the concerns about and debates on this way of working. It has particularly indicated that when working in such teams practitioners may feel pulled in different directions. Most obviously they may feel different obligations and accountability to their professional team and group than they do to the multidisciplinary group in which they are working. This is a common problem that needs to be talked about and worked through.

The growing interest in interprofessional education led to the formation in 1987 of the the Centre for the Advancement of Interprofessional Education in Primary Health and Community Care (CAIPE). CAIPE was the first organisation to promote development, practice and research in shared learning. It has continued to promote shared learning and provides support for those offering it. It collects and disseminates information, helps with networking, organises conferences, commissions and conducts research and publishes a twice-yearly bulletin. Further information can be obtained by writing to CAIPE at 344 Gray's Inn Road, London, WC1X 8BP.

☐ Further reading

DoH, *Building Bridges* (London: DoH, 1995). This is a guide to interagency work in the care and protection of people with serious mental health problems.

A. Loxley, *Collaboration in Health and Welfare* (London: Jessica Kingsley, 1997). This book provides a framework for collaboration and details skills that can be used to facilitate the process.

☐ *World Wide Web sites*

It is worth looking at the Department of Health's web site. Choose a recent policy document and study what it has to say on interprofessional working:

http://www.open.gov.uk/doh/dhhome.htm

The Sainsbury Centre for Mental Health has information on mental health services at

http://www.SainsburyCentre.org.uk

■ *Chapter 6* ■

Social Support and Community Care

Chapter summary
This chapter covers: • The relationship between social support and health. • The importance of support for practitioners. • What networks are and how they are measured. • Different types of network and community care practice. • Working with networks in community care practice.

■ Introduction

Chapter 2 explored the role of carers in community care and introduced the idea of interweaving informal and formal care. Chapter 4 emphasised the importance of this within care management and of the need to have good knowledge of the support being given by informal carers. This chapter develops this discussion by looking at the concepts of social support and support networks. It argues that health and social care practitioners need to work with these support networks in a sensitive and constructive way.

This chapter draws on a tradition of intervention that involves identifying, supporting, developing and extending the support networks of the service user. This tradition has sometimes been called the ecological perspective. Real skills are required for assessing networks and working with them in a sensitive way. Support systems and support networks vary according to divisions of class, gender, sexuality, race and age. Skills in and knowledge of anti-oppressive practice are important in these situations because it it is important not to put more pressure on women to care or reinforce the myth that black people and ethnic minority groups 'look after their own'. Thus a commitment to redress the inequalities and discrimination that occur within services and within society must be a part of this approach.

'Community' is a much contested term. One author has identified 94 different definitions (Hillery, 1955). It can be used to describe a group of people in the same situation (for example the elderly residents of a residential home) or people with something in common (for example the gay community). Probably still the most common use of the word relates to geographical area. Chapter 2 noted that in the early 1980s, government publications moved from talking about care *in* the community to care *by* the community and this distinction was incorporated into official policy (DHSS, 1981, p. 3).

Neither care *by* the community nor care *in* the community is really a tenable choice. The aspiration should be towards care *with* the community (Froland *et al.*, 1981, p. 165). Collins and Pancoast (1976, p. 178) believe that 'care *with* the community is the most viable and productive direction for the future development of human services'. Both this chapter and the next discuss some ways in which this can be done.

■ Social support and health outcomes

Cassel (1974) and Cobb (1976) brought together evidence that the health outcomes of people who experience high levels of stress vary according to level of support or access to support. Caplan (1974a, 1974b) is well known for developing and furthering these ideas in the mental health field. This early work led to many studies of and action projects on the health-protecting functions of social support. There is now a very considerable body of literature on the subject (for example Cohen and Syme, 1985; Taylor, 1993; Ell, 1996; Cooper *et al.*, 1999), and according to the White Paper *Saving Lives: Our Healthier Nation*, 'There is increasing evidence, including from the World Health Organisation, that having strong social networks benefits health' (DoH, 1999b, para. 10.21).

In order to illustrate this let us use a fictional example of an elderly couple, Mr and Mrs McDonald. They are both in their eighties and have lived together for 55 years. Mr McDonald dies suddenly of a heart attack. Because of their long and close relationship this is a very serious life event for Mrs McDonald. Her bereavement may result in serious emotional distress and illness, a situation that is familiar to workers with elderly people and is shown diagrammatically in Figure 6.1.

There are a number of factors that explain why one person copes better with a serious life event than another. Personality characteristics are one

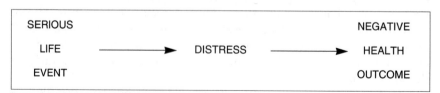

Figure 6.1   *Life events and health outcomes*

such factor. Another, which is the concern of this chapter, is the degree of social support available. For example in Mrs McDonald's case the existence of social support may help relieve her distress about the death of her husband. Furthermore her distress may not have a negative health outcome if there is a support network to help her through the period of grief and mourning. This is illustrated in Figure 6.2, which shows the 'stress-buffering' effect of social support. At the two ends of a spectrum, Mrs McDonald may have virtually no support or she may have a good supportive network comprising a range of relatives, neighbours and friends.

A number of studies give credence to the buffering role of social support (Gottlieb, 1983; Stewart, 1993; Cooper *et al.*, 1999). There is also evidence that social support has a positive effect on health in general (Gottlieb, 1983; Stewart, 1993), in that it fosters good health and good morale by fulfilling basic social needs. Thus if Mrs McDonald has had a good supportive network around her for many years she will be in a healthier state and in better shape to cope with the distress of the bereavement than would otherwise be the case. As Litwin (1995, p. 156) states 'As is widely established in the literature, the informal social network can serve as an effective means of mitigating stress in a range of situations'.

Social support can of course come from different sources – both informal and formal. Family, friends and neighbours are the main source of most people's support. However an elderly person such as Mrs McDonald may also obtain support from a range of other sources, for example good neighbour schemes, day centres, voluntary organisations, workers from the health or social services or the local mosque, temple or church. It is possible to represent these sources of support as a circle around the person as shown in Figure 6.3.

A key issue for health and social care workers is assessing the available

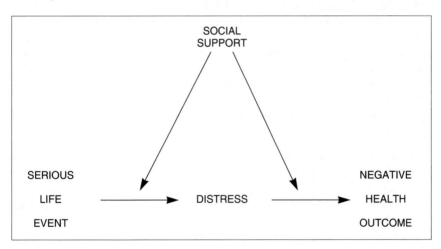

Figure 6.2 *The stress-buffering effects of social support*

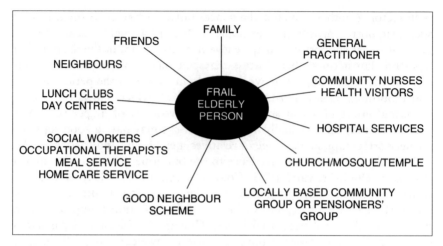

Figure 6.3   *Circle of support for a frail older person*

support and intervening in a way that maximises such support for vulnerable people. One way in which social support can be looked at is in terms of 'networks'. This will be examined in more detail later in the chapter but Figure 6.3 provides a starting point.

■ The importance of social support for practitioners

Familiarity with the vehicles of social support is necessary for nurses because so much care is provided by the informal sector, because of the importance of the self-help and user movement and because of the increasing emphasis within nursing on health promotion and disease prevention. In *Integrating Social Support in Nursing* Stewart (1993) details the links between social support, social networks and health. She applies social support to the four stages of decision-making in nursing – assessment, planning, intervention and evaluation.

Stewart outlines a nursing approach based on social support where users and carers are viewed as partners and allies. She stresses a collaborative approach that goes beyond rhetoric to the need for a detailed analysis of the support network:

> If you say your practice includes assessment of the social network prior to discharge of a patient, state exactly what you will assess: size? frequency of contact? degree of conflict? density? satisfaction? perceived available support? If you determine a social support deficit or disfunction, be specific about its indicators and, if appropriate, your planned intervention (Tilden in Stewart, 1993, p. 204).

Stewart draws on a large body of literature to show the importance of support networks for health outcomes and makes a powerful argument in favour of nurses knowing about and working constructively with support networks. The need for knowledge about and skills in networking applies to all workers in the broad area of health promotion (Trevillion, 1999).

Social support is important for social workers for the same reasons as it is for nurses. In the history of social work it is possible to trace periods when theorists and practitioners have stressed social work as being rooted in the community and support networks. However at other times the focus of theory and practice has been more on casework and therapy with the individual and her or his family. In the 1960s the Seebohm Report (1968) emphasised the contribution of the community, and of practice within that context.

In the early 1980s the Barclay Committee was asked by the government to investigate the role and function of social work. The ensuing Barclay Report (1982) advocated that community social work should rest 'upon a recognition that the majority of social care in England and Wales is provided, not by the statutory or voluntary social service agencies but by individual citizens who are often linked into informal caring networks' (ibid., p 205).

The report emphasised the importance of working with user networks, although its idea of a network was vague and ill-defined. It called for a partnership between informal caring networks and formal social service organisations. It defined 'community' as 'a network or networks of informal relationships between people connected with each other by kinship, common interests, geographical proximity, friendship, occupation, or the giving and receiving of services – or various combinations of these' (ibid., p. 199). The report acknowledged that the bulk of social care was provided by ordinary people in networks and argued that social workers needed to find ways to link into these informal networks and work with them. Social workers were described as 'upholders of networks', whose task was to 'enable, empower, support and encourage, but not usually to take over from social networks . . . . Clients, relations, neighbours and volunteers become partners with the social worker in developing and providing social care networks' (ibid., p. 209). During the 1980s there was an upsurge in community social work, which involved working closely with and developing local support networks.

A call for partnership can also be found in the Griffiths Report on community care: 'Families, friends, neighbours and other local people provide the majority of care in response to needs which they are uniquely well placed to identify and respond to. This will continue to be the primary means by which people are enabled to live normal lives in community settings' (Griffiths, 1988, p. 5). The influential report took this as its starting point, and recommended that publicly provided services should support and where possible strengthen these networks of carers (ibid., p 5).

In the 1990s social service authorities developed organisational structures for implementing the new legislation on children and adults. Many created separate structures and separate teams for children and families' and for 'adults'. The community social work ideas and practice of the mid and late 1980s faltered under these pressures. Likewise the practice of neighbourhood nursing flourished less well under the new 'trust' arrangements for nursing brought in during the 1990s with most district nursing staff being attached to GP practices (Audit Commission, 1999).

Historically nursing and social workers seem to have blown hot and cold at different times over their relations with communities/local networks. There is almost a cyclical pattern to this. Earlier chapters have stressed how during the 1990s, due to the legislative changes and the impact of internal markets, pressure was put on practitioners to undertake individual work, with less attention to community/network factors. The emphasis during the 1990s of 'targeting those in greatest need' contributed to this loss of emphasis on support networks. However this was balanced by government rhetoric on and acknowledgement of the role played in community care by informal carers (DoH, 1989a). Thus practitioners again found themselves in an ambivalent situation, with competing pressures and tensions.

■ Strategies for partnership

One of the most useful attributes among community health and social care workers is the ability is to identify, work with and enlarge service users' networks of support. Collins and Pancoast (1976) in their book on neighbourhood-based forms of informal support argued that natural helping networks were of great potential use in social welfare. Here the focus was on mutual aid, linking up with and making use of 'central figures' or 'natural neighbours'.

Biegel *et al.* (1984) developed this in relation to network approaches to working with older people. Froland *et al.* (1981) looked at strategies that agencies might adopt in order to maximise partnership. The focus here was on interweaving the work of welfare agencies and the informal sector. As noted in Chapter 2 there were others, such as Bayley (1973) and Bulmer (1987), who stressed the need for interweaving and partnership in their writing. Froland *et al.* (1981) suggested five strategies for welfare agencies that are still very relevant when considering care in the community.

□ *Personal networks strategy*

Once the details of a network are known there may be different ways in which it can be modified to suit the user. Members of the network may hold meetings in order better to coordinate their activities. Sometimes it is possible to improve the functioning of the network. At other times it may be better to try to create new networks. If a worker is trying to help someone join a network then one of the following strategies may help.

☐ *Volunteer linking*

There is a long tradition of voluntary welfare work. An example here is the Buddy Service, which provides friendship and support for people with HIV/AIDS. This was started by the Terence Higgins Trust in London but similar schemes have been set up throughout the UK. A Buddy is a volunteer who commits him or herself to befriending someone with HIV/AIDS and sees them perhaps two or three times a week. Training is given and each Buddy receives advice on befriending, listening and practical tasks.

☐ *Mutual aid networks*

There are a vast number of self-help organisations and groups. This type of help can be very powerful because all the members have had similar experiences. One of the oldest and best known is Alcoholics Anonymous. More recently self-advocacy groups have been set up for people with learning difficulties.

☐ *Neighbourhood helper strategy*

In any area there are usually a number of local people who take on a neighbourly helping role. This strategy involves the agency finding out who these people are and working with them. There may be occasions when they need support, but there may also be occasions when they can generate support and help for a vulnerable person through their local contacts and by virtue of their local leadership.

☐ *Community empowerment strategy*

This is similar to mutual aid but usually involves a worker helping groups and communities to organise mutual aid, self-help and local empowerment. Because it involves collective organisation it is especially important as a strategy against oppressive structures and policies.

Often these strategies can be beneficially combined. The above categorisation into five strategies remains useful for looking at the different ways in which the formal sector can relate to the informal sector. There is a great deal of altruism within the community, and health and social care workers need to work with this and encourage it (Titmus, 1973) whilst endeavouring not to exploit people. Reflect on these strategies in relation to the case study in Box 6.1.

Box 6.1   *Case study – application of partnership strategies*

Peter Harris has a learning difficulty and has been in a long-stay hospital for 15 years. He is being moved with two other people to a small group home 12 miles from the hospital. When Peter is discharged from hospital his network is likely to be dramatically changed. People who spend many years in hospital build up a network associated with the institution. In Peter's case that network will be fractured, prompting two important questions:

• Will anyone help him to keep in touch with the old network if he wishes to?
• Will he be able to build a new network up in his new situation?

In the interest of good care management practice the maintenance of Peter's network will need to be actively worked at. A number of the partnership strategies described above may be relevant. He may need help with keeping in touch with people who have been important to him. Within his new community, linking him to a citizen advocacy scheme may be one way of helping him to build a network in his new situation (volunteer linking). Citizen advocacy is sometimes described as 'lending people networks'. This means linking someone to Peter as an advocate. Subsequently the members of the advocate's network will get to know Peter and in this way a network is 'lent'. There may be a self-advocacy group that Peter can join (mutual aid networks). A worker may help Peter and others to play an active role in their new area (community empowerment). Mention is made in Chapter 7 of 'circles of support' and 'support tenants', both of which link closely to this discussion of networks and could be applicable to Peter.

■ What is meant by network?

'Network' is often used interchangeably with 'support' but it also has a more precise definition, drawing from the methodology of network analysis in the social sciences. Network analysis is a research strategy and a sophisticated way of analysing relationships. It is generally considered to have its origins in social anthropology. Barnes (1954) used the network concept to describe fishing villagers who had organised groups across both kinship and social class boundaries. Bott (1957) used the idea of network in her study of London families and marital network patterns. Network analysis developed further in anthropology in the late 1960s and early 1970s with such studies as Mayer's *Tribesmen or Townsmen* (1961), Mitchell's *Social Networks in Urban Situations* (1969), Barnes' *Social Networks* (1972) and Boissevain and Mitchell's *Network Analysis: Studies In Human Interaction* (1973).

For those living at home and experiencing increased incapacity there are important questions about what sort of network they have, how it changes and whether it can cope with increasing demand. Some of the ideas of network analysis can be helpful for practitioners in relation both to the analysis of situations and to practice. Many people stay in the community because their networks are sufficiently strong to cope with the demands. It is often because networks can no longer cope that admission to residential, nursing home or hospital care is required. It is also worth bearing in mind that not all network links are supportive. As a way of understanding what networks are and making them more real for yourself, carry out the exercise in Box 6.2.

Box 6.2   Drawing up a network

On a large sheet of paper draw a circle with yourself in the middle. Around yourself write the names of those with whom you have a relationship and to whom you could turn for help and support. Those who are closest to you should be placed nearest the centre. Do this before you read on.

- How many people have you put in your personal network? This is called the network *size*.
- How is your network made up in relation to divisions such as friends, neighbours and colleagues? This is called the network *composition*.
- How well do the people in your network know each other? This is called the network *density*. (If they know each other well it is a high density network. If they do not know each other well it is a low density network.)

Networks can be very different. In the centre of the network in Figure 6.4 is the recently bereaved Mrs McDonald who was introduced at the beginning of the chapter. She is frail, partially sighted and has a number of medical problems. She has a network size of four: her son, who lives over a hundred miles away and visits about every three months, or more often in a crisis; a daily home help; an Age Concern 'good neighbour'; and a nextdoor neighbour. They all know each other well so there is a high density. This means that when a difficulty arises they are quickly in touch with each other and cooperate to provide appropriate help or support.

Contrast this network with the network diagram in Figure 6.5. This network has the same composition but none of the people know each other (there is a low density) and they do not communicate with each other. (In reality this is unlikely but it illustrates the contrast with Figure 6.4.) It is much harder to see how Mrs McDonald could survive in the community with so little cooperation between those who support her. The members of the network would not cover the gaps or back each other up when there were problems.

In a situation such as this it might be helpful to organise a network meeting. With the user's permission the central members of the network are drawn together for a discussion. This meeting can help clarify who is

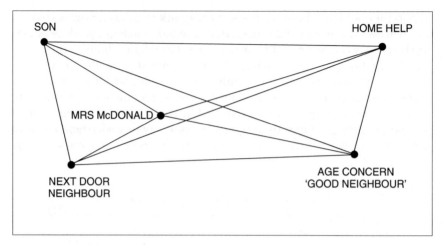

Figure 6.4   *A high density network*

doing what; identify any weak parts of the network and help the network members to link up and get to know each other. People who have never met or coordinated their efforts may begin to do so. In this way an effective interweaving of formal and informal care can be achieved. Some key questions to pose in relation to practice are as follows:

- Is there a good reason for convening the meeting?
- Has the practitioner prepared well for the meeting and does he or she know the reasons for it?
- Has the user been fully involved in the discussions about the meeting and who is invited? The user normally attends unless there is a good reason why this should not be the case.

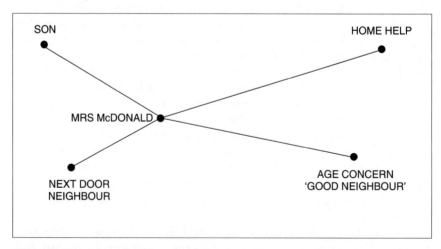

Figure 6.5   *A low density network*

- Is the meeting likely to be constructive? If one of the network members is, for example, very negative for whatever reason, it may not be helpful to have the meeting.

■ The nature of the network

This section provides ideas on how to work out the details of networks as a practitioner. The following exercise requires you to choose someone who is already being worked with, preferably a frail, older person. The idea is to try to find out about his or her network. Write down who helps the person in question, if anyone, with practical tasks such as:

- Cleaning the house
- Cooking
- Washing dishes
- Laundry
- Gardening
- Household repairs
- Household decorations
- Shopping
- Pension collection
- Transportation

List who helps, if anyone, with personal care tasks such as:

- Bathing
- Washing
- Dressing
- Going to the toilet
- Getting into bed
- Feeding
- Shaving/hair combing
- Cutting toenails
- Negotiating steps/stairs
- Getting around the house
- Getting out of doors

Ask the person in question the following questions on

- Who can you confide in about problems?
- Who would you call real friends?
- Who depends on your friendship?
- Who do you keep in touch with over the telephone?

This is a quick way of obtaining an idea of the people in someone's network. The checklist is particularly applicable to frail older people. For other people it may well have to be modified. Having drawn up the list, show it to the person and ask them if there is anyone not on the list who gives help and support.

Adding up the list gives the *size* of the person's network. The *composition* is determined by whether the people on it are from the formal sector (social worker, GP, community nurse) or the informal sector (friends, neighbours). The *density* of the network depends on the extent to which those in the network know each other. In practical terms this can be determined by listing the network members along the top and down the side of a sheet of paper. 'Does X know Y?' is asked in relation to each possible relationship (Fischer, 1982).

It needs to be said that examining someone's personal network is just one way of measuring support, and the method of measuring the network described above is only one way of doing this. However the practice of obtaining names from the person and asking about those names is common.

Returning to the exercise, the size, composition and an idea of the density of the person's network have now been established. Taking each member of the network individually, is there anything else it would be interesting to know about them? It could be important to ask the person concerned the following questions:

- How often do you see them? (Frequency)
- How long have you known them? (Duration)
- How far away do they live? (Proximity)
- How close do they feel to the person? (Closeness)
- How prominent or important is the person in the network? (Prominence) (Sharkey, 1989)

The answers to these questions need to be considered as a whole. In some cases, for example, the person concerned may not get on very well with a relative who lives nearby and visits often, but feels close to and able to discuss things with a relative who lives some distance away but keeps in touch by phone.

There are a range of other questions that could be asked to help fill out the picture of the person's network. Once you have the network map (it is a good idea to draw it as a diagram) you and the person concerned might be able to identify aspects that might helpfully be changed.

■ Different types of network

It will have become clear that practitioners need to go beyond simply saying that they acknowledge the value of informal care and will work with it. They need a knowledge of how it works, how it varies and the implications of that variation for practice. They need to know how to assess it and how to link their intervention or care packages most effectively to it.

Wenger's (1994) work on the types of network that exist is helpful in developing this knowledge and skill. She argues that different patterns of informal support exist in the community and that different types of neighbourhood produce different types of network and different patterns of help-seeking behaviour. Certain aspects of help or support networks have been identified as crucial (Wenger and Day, 1995):

- How close the network members live to one another.
- How many members know each other.
- Which informal sources are turned to for help.

In her study of older people in North Wales, Wenger (1984) found that support networks had an average of five to seven members, although the range was from two to 22. She developed a measurement instrument for practitioner identification of network type and tested the usefulness of this as a practice tool. Five types of support network were identified on the basis of the following factors:

- Local availability of close kin.
- Level of involvement of family, friends and neighbours.
- Level of interaction with the community and voluntary groups.

The networks are named according to the nature of the older person's relationship to the network. The first three types are based on the presence of local kin, the other two reflect their absence:

- Family dependent.
- Local integrated.
- Local self-contained.
- Wider community focused.
- Private restricted.

Wenger argues that different types of network make different demands on the statutory services. For example the level of domiciliary care required differs according to network type. Network types themselves change over time. At different times communities have differing proportions of network types, with likely implications for the services provided. Only some networks can adapt to support highly dependent older people in need of long-term care.

When older people have problems or needs, how they are responded to and how they are met depends on the type of network available. Wenger discusses this in relation to problems resulting from impaired mobility, illness, hospital discharge, the impact of widowhood, isolation and loneliness, dementia/mental illness. She also indicates how different network types are likely to perceive and use services such as home care, meals, good neighbour schemes, community nursing, day care, respite care and residential care (Wenger and Day, 1995).

The key message from Wenger's work is that practitioners need to work to support or complement the existing networks. Workers should not simply consider the person concerned, her or his problems and the available services when designing a care package. They should also take full account of the support network, and knowledge of the network type can assist with the planning of services.

Other attempts have been made to develop network typologies. For example Litwin has related the different network types available to older people in Israel to the use of health services (Litwin, 1997), health status (Litwin, 1998) and the use of both formal and informal help (Litwin, 1999).

■ Working with networks in community care practice

It is often because the informal network is under great strain that a situation is brought to the attention of the formal services. The services need to have some sense of how the network is working before a decision is made on the way forward. In their evaluation of the Kent Community Care Scheme, Challis and Davies (1986, p. 1) state that, 'an integrated system of care for a frail, elderly person will not happen spontaneously; rather it has to be consciously created. The active building, support and maintenance of a support network requires the development of effective case management with the frail elderly to ensure the coordination and performance of care tasks'.

In the Kent scheme whole networks sometimes had to be constructed and fragile networks reinforced, and in all cases an effort was made to improve communication between the different parts of the network (ibid., p. 223). This means that a conscious effort was made to increase the density of the network. In the evaluation of the project there is acknowledgement that networks are fragile and that inappropriate formal intervention can cause informal carers to give up.

Litwin (1995) outlines four models of network intervention, although he acknowledges that in practice they overlap and are not distinct. These are:

- Network therapy: this draws on the perspectives of family therapy.
- Network mediation: this might involve, for example, expanding networks and increasing the connections between them.
- Network construction: this involves building a network where none or only a very small one exists.
- Network reinforcement: here a network under strain receives support or back-up from the paid services. This is similar to the notion employed by some writers and practitioners of interweaving informal and formal care.

There is some tradition of working with networks rather than just individuals, and a history of practice in different countries to draw on (Trimble and Kliman, 1995). Pioneers of this approach in the United States include Attneave (1969), Rueveni (1979) and Speck (Speck and Attneave, 1973).

Mention has been made of changing the density of a network by, for example, convening a meeting or a series of meetings of those involved within the network. Networks can be very fragile and the meetings may reveal that there is a need for the support and maintenance of informal carers. Perhaps those at the meetings will help to provide this, or alternatives may be explored. It may become clear that the network is too small. The size of a network might be increased by recruiting a volunteer or a good neighbour. Advocates for people with learning disabilities or people who are mentally distressed often add to the size of networks through mutual involvement in ordinary leisure activities.

Heron (1998) applies similar ideas in her study of carers. She describes the valuable role that support groups can play for carers and suggests that carers may benefit from an improvement of their social networks. She suggests two stages for the latter – first the mapping of the existing network (similar to the method described above) and then a discussion of options for developing the network using new and existing contacts.

Network therapy is one of the approaches used for treating people who abuse alcohol and drugs (Galanter, 1999). Family members and friends are involved in the treatment so that they can provide support and promote a change of attitude. One function of Alcoholics Anonymous is to provide a support network of people who are committed to giving up alcohol. Replacing a 'drinking network' with a network of people who are determined to stop drinking can be a crucial step along the road to recovery.

Social networks shape high-risk behaviour and thus the spread of HIV. Friedman's (1999) study shows that social networks are of vital importance in understanding and fighting HIV/AIDs. Understanding networks is thus important in this and other areas of preventive health care.

Practice in community care needs to be based on a careful analysis of the current support available from both the formal and the informal sector in order to achieve a sensible and sensitive interweaving of care. Herein lie some of the real skills of care management as the process is not cold and technocratic but rather demands considerable assessment and intervention skills. There will be some situations where the current network is very limited and fragile and a considerable input of formal services will be needed. However there will be other situations where the activities of the current network can simply be modified to meet needs. Sometimes, for example, the provision of appropriate guidance, training or reassurance by district nurses to carers may be all that is required. Intervention by practitioners will vary according to the assessment but could be directed at:

- Strengthening the current support system.
- Creating a new support system.

- Training users in the skills necessary to help them strengthen their own support system.

■ Practice issues

This chapter has discussed the links between life events, social support and health outcomes. It is important for health and social care workers to appreciate the importance of informal care and to work constructively with it. One way of doing this is to think, analyse and intervene on the basis of networks. Networks are an important aspect of coping with life crises, coping with deteriorating health and continuing to live in the community. Thus key tasks for care managers are to:

- assess the users' current support networks, and
- take action to ensure that the support networks continue, with appropriate assistance.

Practitioners can make best use of this chapter by working with service users to assess their networks so that any agreed intervention or way forward can be informed by this background knowledge. It is an appropriate approach for a wide range of service users (Whittaker and Garbarino, 1983).

Network analysis is helpful for the care manager in terms of analysing the current network and assisting with sorting out how the successful interweaving of formal and informal care can take place. It is acknowledged that this may be difficult if there is pressure for a quick assessment from a practitioner on the purchasing side of the purchaser/provider divide. Where agencies are able to implement policies aimed at prevention the approach is especially valuable.

It is useful for practioners to reflect on the following (Wenger, 1994):

- People with different types of network are likely to make different degrees and types of demand on statutory services.
- Knowledge and understanding of the various types of support network can be a useful tool for community care practitioners at the level of the individual and the team.

The telephone has been enormously beneficial in respect of maintaining networks and enabling people to obtain support when needed. In the future it may be that communication through the internet will become increasingly important in developing support networks and obtaining support.

☐ *Further reading*

M. Bulmer, *The Social Basis of Community Care* (London: Allen & Unwin, 1987). This is an excellent introduction to some of the sociological debates that under-pin community care. It has a chapter on social networks and another on inter-weaving formal and informal care.

H. Cooper, S. Arber, L. Fee and J. Ginn, *The Influence of Social Support and Social Capital on Health* (London: HEA, 1999). This study includes a review of the literature on the links between health, health behaviour and social support.

S. Trevillion, *Networking and Community Partnership* (Aldershot: Ashgate, 1999). This book applies networking ideas to a number of areas, including assessment, empowerment and care management.

G. C. Wenger, *Support Networks of Older People: A Guide for Practitioners*, (Bangor: Centre for Social Policy Research and Development, University of Wales, 1994). This guide provides a detailed explanation of Wenger's typology, her assessment form and ideas on intervention.

■ *Chapter 7* ■

User Empowerment and Community Care

Chapter summary

This chapter:

- Discusses some key influences on empowerment in community care, including the independent living movement, the social model of disability, normalisation and ordinary living, anti-racist and anti-oppressive ideas, the self-help and user movement, and community development.
- Outlines two models of empowerment and describes a 'ladder of empowerment'.
- Situates community care in a wider context and considers debates on social exclusion and regeneration.

■ Introduction

Previous chapters have referred to the recognition of user empowerment in the community care changes of the 1990s. It has been pointed out (for example in Chapter 4) that this has often conflicted with other objectives, including the rationing of services and the provision of services within tight budgets. This chapter will explore the welcome emphasis on empowerment, but this needs to be considered in the wider context that includes the often complex and varied expectations that practitioners have to meet.

One of the three fundamental aims of *Caring for People*, was to 'give people a greater individual say in how they live their lives and the services they need to help them to do so' (DoH, 1989a, p. 4). Later practice guidance from the Department of Health gave further emphasis to involving users and increasing their choice, using the language of empowerment:

> The rationale for this reorganisation is the empowerment of users and carers. Instead of users and carers being subordinate to the wishes of service providers, the roles will be progressively adjusted. In this way, users and carers will be enabled to exercise the same power as consumers of other services. This redressing of the balance of power is the best guarantee of a continuing improvement in the quality of service (DoH, 1991a, p. 9).

The aspects of user empowerment that were built into the community care changes can be summarised as follows:

- Users to receive better information about services and procedures.
- Each social service authority would set up a complaints procedure for users.
- There would be consultation with users in relation to community care plans.
- Assessment of individuals would be guided by the needs of the user.

Although the changes were useful in themselves in practice they only had a limited impact on empowerment. The empowerment envisaged was mainly strengthening the individual's right to (1) complain, (2) better information and (3) needs-led assessment. The scope for collective organisation was limited to participation in community care plans and whatever could be made of the general rhetoric of user empowerment.

From the above it is clear that there was limited government encouragement of user empowerment. However a variety of other influences on community care have had a greater impact on real empowerment. Foremost amongst these are:

- The independent living movement.
- The influence of the social model of disability.
- Ideas about normalisation, ordinary living and supported living.
- The emphasis on anti-racist and anti-oppressive practice.
- The continuing development of the user movement and self-help groups.
- The influence of community work ideas and practices.

All these have influenced the development of good practice. However, practitioners have also had to struggle with resource constraints, which frequently serve to limit empowerment. The first six sections of this chapter will outline each of these influences in turn.

■ Independent living movement

In the United States during the 1960s discrimination was identified as a major problem in relation to black people, women and disabled people. Disability thus became an issue of concern to the civil rights movement. The links between oppressed groups were made more explicit in the United States than in the United Kingdom. The movement of disabled people in the United States has sometimes been called the Independent Living Movement and there have been examples of disabled people taking service provision into their own hands, for instance the first Centre For Independent Living was set up in Berkeley, California, in 1972 (Crewe and Zola, 1983). Other centres were opened during the subsequent years. A central aim was to 'demedicalise' disability, that is, to put a stop to disability being treated as akin to sickness.

The movement has been slower to develop in the United Kingdom. It had its origins in people's attempts to leave residential care and live independently in the community. Examples of important initiatives are the Derbyshire Centre for Integrated Living, the Hampshire Centre for Independent Living and the West of England Centre for Integrated Living. The Derbyshire Centre for Integrated Living, which was set up in the early 1980s, is run and managed by disabled people for disabled people and its mission is 'to secure independent, integrated living opportunities for disabled people in order to promote their full participation in the mainstream of economic life in Derbyshire'. The centre offers a range of services such as peer counselling, help and information, and a wheelchair repair and maintenance scheme. Further details of its history and development are described by Priestley (1999).

According to Jenny Morris (1993) the philosophy of the independent living movement is based on the following assumptions: that all human life is of value; that anyone, whatever their impairment, is capable of making choices; that people who are disabled by society's reaction to physical, intellectual and sensory impairment and emotional distress have the right to assert control over their lives; and that disabled people have the right to participate fully in society (ibid., p. 21).

Independent disabled people (as in the independent living movement) argue that they are in charge of decision making even if they do not do all the tasks themselves (for example, getting washed and dressed). The reversal of the power relationship is achieved by moving away from disabled people being controlled by personal assistance (however kind and well-meaning) towards control over the type and timing of the personal assistance they receive. That is, disabled people themselves decide which services they want (such as help with getting up, going to bed, eating) and when they want them. The physical inability to do certain tasks should not lead to loss of control and choice. What is important is the nature of the relationship with the person who is doing the tasks. This relates to who is in charge of what is done, how it is done and when it is done. Obviously there can be tensions between this philosophy and the way in which caring has been done in the past by many carers – both formal and informal. This potential and real conflict was brought out at the end of Chapter 2 and practitioners may experience conflicting pressures between the aspirations of disabled people and the concerns of carers.

The setting up by the UK government of the Independent Living Fund (ILF) in 1988 gave a boost to the independent living movement. Disabled people who could meet the assessment criteria were given a regular grant that enabled them to employ people to help them live independently. Hence the fund gave disabled people control over their own care by enabling them to employ the carers of their choice and tell them what to do. This was very different from having to accept the dictates and organisation of the local home care and nursing service. Power shifted to the disabled person. In this way the fund fed into the aims of the Independent Living Movement and provided a vision of how user-led and user-controlled care packages could be set up to meet the real needs of disabled people.

The community care changes in the early 1990s led to the closure of the Independent Living Fund in March 1993. By then 21 500 disabled users were receiving regular payments. The ILF was replaced by two new trusts:

- The Independent Living (Extension) Fund was set up as a charitable trust in order to continue payments to existing claimants.
- The Independent Living (1993) Fund works in partnership with local authorities to devise joint care packages. The fund provides a top-up to council services. Applicants have to be of working age and be able to show that without help they would have to go into residential care.

The loss of the ILF in its original form provoked a great deal of anger amongst disabled people as it had provided them with greater control over their own lives as well as independence, and for many its removal meant a real reduction in possibilities for empowerment. During the early 1990s there was a lot of pressure on the government by organisations of disabled people to legislate on direct payments and this pressure eventually bore fruit with the passing of Community Care (Direct Payments) Act 1996. The Act gave local authorities the power to make direct payments, but not the duty to do so. Service users may ask carers or other third parties to handle and manage the payments but the user must remain in control of the arrangements and is accountable for the way in which the money is used. It is stressed that direct payments are intended to facilitate independent living, not to switch from dependence on the local authority to dependence on another party. The local authority has discretion over whether to offer someone direct payments and can decide whether they are appropriate and whether the disabled person can manage them (DoH, 1997c). The Labour government has expressed support for the further development of direct payment schemes, extending them to all adults (DoH, 1998a). Direct payments schemes are a result of much lobbying and pressure over many years and a wide variety of personal assistance schemes have been developed by disabled people (Priestley, 1999).

■ Social model of disability

People involved in the independent living movement have often used the social model of disability as a theoretical perspective. The two influences on empowerment are intertwined.

A model is a simplified version of how things operate and can help make sense of a complicated situation. Two models can be used to explain how disability is regarded by society. The first is the 'individual model', in which a disabled person is seen as having to adjust to society. (This model is sometimes called the medical model, the traditional model or the personal tragedy model.) Central aspects of this model are that disability is viewed as a 'tragic' situation; individuals have to adapt to their impairment; individuals have to adapt to fit into society; and disabled people may be seen as either objects of pity or heroes (Oliver and Sapey, 1999).

In contrast, under the 'social oppression model' society is expected to adjust to the disabled person. This model is advocated by a number of disabled persons' organisations and writers (for example Oliver 1990, 1996). From this perspective disabled people are seen primarily as an oppressed group, prevented from achieving their full potential by the structures and ideologies/discourses of society. Society 'disables' individuals both by creating environmental obstacles and by its attitude towards them. Disabled people have the same range of needs and feelings as other people but society restricts their access to public transport, entertainment and public places as well as education and employment. According to this approach action should be taken to enable disabled people to play a full and equal part in all aspects of life.

These two models simplify complex situations but they nevertheless have fundamental implications for disabled people, their carers and the organisation of services provided for them. The model adopted will affect how practitioners behave and the way in which they practice. It is probable that most people have been heavily influenced by a portrayal of disability that conforms largely to the first model and is constantly reinforced by the media and some charities.

The social model does not stress the restrictions created by impairments, but rather the restrictions created by a society geared to able-bodied people. It shows how society denies disabled people the means to do what they are capable of doing. Hence the problem is not the impaired individual but the disabling society. This model emphasises the need to identify the way in which the structures and institutions of society further disable people with disabilities so that these disabling structures can be challenged. The social model celebrates difference and relates especially to people with a physical or sensory impairment.

Proponents of the social model have been critical of those involved in the 'rehabilitation' services for medicalising the rehabilitation process (Nocon and Baldwin, 1998). Health and social care workers in rehabilitation services have had to rethink their practices as a result of these criticisms. This also applies in respect of the influence of the ideas of normalisation.

■ Normalisation, ordinary living and supported living

Normalisation has been especially influential in relation to services for people with learning difficulties, an area of provision in which the social model of disability has had only a limited impact (Stalker *et al.*, 1999). In the past people with learning difficulties were often shut away in large hospitals as a result of policies of physical exclusion and segregation. The ideas of 'normalisation' grew as a way of combating segregation and integrating people with learning difficulties back into society. Its origins were in Denmark in the late 1950s and the ideas influenced the provision of services in Denmark and Sweden in the 1960s. In the United States, during the 1970s and 1980s Wolf Wolfensberger (1972) proposed and then developed more elaborate ideas on normalisation, which he later referred to as 'social role valorisation'. This is his preferred description but the word 'normalisation' is still commonly used.

The aim of normalisation is simply to treat all people as equal citizens, with equal rights and equal access to valued social roles. The ideas of normalisation are applied to groups of people who have been regarded as of lesser value and suggest how to change that situation. Members of such groups are likely to be treated unfairly and unjustly, thus discrimination is one consequence of being devalued.

A vicious circle can be set up in which people who are seen and treated as being of lesser value come to believe it themselves. That is, when people hear negative views about themselves and experience negative behaviour, then over time they come to accept that view of themselves. Another word for this is 'internalisation'. Normalisation is one tool for identifying, analysing and breaking the circle that traps various groups of people into maintaining poor views of themselves and discourages their aspiration to be valued members of society. This can happen to people who are elderly, people who have a physical, sensory or learning disability and people with mental health problems. Thus the ideas of normalisation are relevant to all adult groups in the field of community care.

Normalisation principles have been a force for change in the United Kingdom, and in particular they have contributed to the 'ordinary life' movement. This movement is based on the conviction that people with severe learning difficulties should live ordinary lives. John O'Brien (King's Fund Centre, 1991) has described the implications of normalisation in relation to what services should try to achieve or accomplish for users. He has identified five major service accomplishments that are a practical application of the 'ordinary life' values for people with learning difficulties (ibid., p. 45):

- Community presence: the right to live and spend their time in the community rather than in residential, day or leisure facilities that segregate them from other members of society.

- Competence: in order for a full and rewarding life to be lived in the local community, many will require help with learning new skills and gaining access to a wider range of activities.
- Choice: a high-quality service will give priority to enhancing the choices available to people and generally protecting their human rights.
- Respect: services can play an important role in helping people to enjoy the same status as other valued members of society.
- Relationships: help and encouragement are needed to enable people with learning difficulties to mix with other non-disabled people in their daily lives.

These have been powerful and radical principles when applied to much of the provision which has been available for people with learning difficulties. Since the 1970s people with learning difficulties have progressed towards living ordinary lives in a whole variety of areas, such as education, housing, employment and leisure. To use a more recent term, normalisation has acted as a powerful tool against social exclusion.

According to some interpretations of normalisation the devalued group is expected to adopt the culture and lifestyle of the dominant group (this process is sometimes called assimilation). However, whilst oppressed groups want to be valued as human beings, they might not wish to follow an approach that sees assimilation as the only goal or assumes that disadvantaged groups should aspire to society's norms (Szivos, 1992, p. 128).

In summary then, whereas the social model acknowledges and celebrates difference, normalisation often emphasises assimilation. Szivos suggests that at a practical level, health and social care workers might ask themselves whether their way of working improves 'the self-concept of [the] client by acknowledging his or her right to feel positively about being different?' (ibid.)

Ideas and practices associated with self-advocacy and citizen advocacy have been greatly influenced by normalisation (Brandon, 1995). Ward's (1999) edited book describes some of the innovations in advocacy and empowerment that have taken place in respect of people with learning difficulties.

Advocacy systems are important in relation to empowerment because an effective system of community care ought to build in more power to the user and an advocacy system is therefore an essential ingredient. However the concept of advocacy or authorised representation is missing from the 1990 Act. The guidance to the 1990 Act encourages representation or advocacy where necessary but it was not built into the actual legislation. Interestingly it was strongly built into the Disabled Persons Act 1986 but these were sections of the Act which the government never implemented.

A further development has been the idea of 'supported living'. This links very much to the themes of Chapter 6 and stresses the importance of networks of people to provide support. Supported living looks at people in context. Among other things this means incorporating the construction of networks into the planning process, retaining and/or rebuilding networks, linking well into the community context and ensuring that the activities of paid staff complement the natural support available (Simons, 1997, p. 40).

In practical terms supported living draws heavily on two devices: circles of support and support tenants. Circles of support are groups of people who meet on a regular basis to help a vulnerable individual achieve his or her goals. The circle comprises family, friends, neighbours and people in the community. 'Circles celebrate diversity rather than minimise difference' (ibid., p. 41). A support tenant is someone who has made a commitment to be around for a person with learning difficulties. This usually means living full-time in the same household and is undertaken for agreed periods of time in exchange for subsidised accommodation, an honorarium or both (ibid.)

Whilst supported living has developed in relation to people with learning difficulties and has links with 'ordinary living' it also links to and has similarities with the Independent Living Movement, which is primarily associated with people with physical impairments. Simons argues that 'The links between the two are likely to be increasingly important, particularly with the passing of the legislation enabling direct payments' (ibid., p. 130).

Whilst independent living, the social model and normalisation have each been powerful influences in themselves, they have often been used eclectically, with the different perspectives being drawn on at different times (Stalker *et al.*, 1999). Hence some organisations have not offered a consistent approach but rather one characterised by some contradiction and conflict (ibid.)

■ Anti-racist and anti-oppressive practice

Chapter 1 noted that questions of race did not figure strongly in reports on community care in the 1970s and 1980s and the subsequent 1990 legislation (Ahmad and Atkin, 1996). Much of the provision was 'colour blind' and influenced by the myth that 'they look after their own'. A colour blind approach means that a service is designed and delivered in the same way for all users. For example, when planning meals on wheels or meals in day care or residential homes no allowance is made for dietary differences between communities and cultures. It is assumed that this service will be equally appropriate for all those who need it, thus ignoring the reality of a multiracial society in which services should be adapted for particular needs. The colour-blind approach of 'we offer the same services to everyone' is inherently discriminatory. Provision really should be needs-led and sensitive to people from black and ethnic minority communities. Where services do not 'fit' there has been a tendency to resort to the myth that 'they look after their own'. This myth has been used by agencies in relation to black people and ethnic minority communities as an excuse for not making necessary changes to their services and expanding the level of service provision. An anti-racist strategy in community care needs to address both of these myths and include the points within Box 7.1 (Sharkey, 1995).

Box 7.1   *Components of an anti-racist strategy*

Any anti-racist strategy in community care should include:

• Methods of actively countering overt and covert (or institutional) racism within health and social care organisations.
• Appreciation of the care being provided within black communities and of the work of black self-help projects.
• Awareness of and methods of countering attitudes that inhibit the provision of appropriate services (colour blindness and the myth that 'they look after their own').
• Recognition that black communities experience more of the controlling aspects of the welfare state and fewer of its beneficial provisions (Skellington, 1992, p. 87).
• Positive action to improve the low take-up of some services.
• Consideration of separate provision for black communities in some situations.
• Recognition that black communities have a right to appropriate community care and that it should not be seen or portrayed as a special privilege.
• Workers to learn from users about their needs and how they wish to be treated.
• Consideration of other social divisions.

Race is just one of several social divisions. Threaded throughout this book have been comments on the impact of divisions such as class, sexuality, age, gender and disability and how these divisions intertwine. There has been much discussion in the social care literature of the impact of social divisions and the development of anti-oppressive practice (Thompson, 1997, 1998). Such values and practice were integrated into social work training during the 1980s and 1990s, raising questions for cohorts of students about whether their practice would lead to empowerment or contribute to further oppression (Dalrymple and Burke, 1995; Braye and Preston-Shoot, 1995). Whilst there has not been the same emphasis within nursing education, some writers in this field have emphasised the impact of structural factors such as discrimination against older people (Thomas, 1999) and against gay and lesbian service users (Godfrey, 1999). These writers stress the need for nursing practitioners actively to challenge ageism and heterosexism.

■ The growth of self-help groups, user groups and movements

There is a long history of self-help and self-organisation amongst users of community care services. The British Deaf Association was formed in 1890 and the National League of the Blind was set up as a trade union in 1899. This rich history can be explored in works such as *Disability Politics* (Campbell and Oliver, 1996). A number of writers describe this history in terms of the development of a social movement (Beresford, 1997; Campbell and Oliver, 1996; Priestley, 1999). Some disabled people see it as a liberation movement (Oliver, 1996). The disability movement has been greatly influenced by the social model of disability and the idea of independent living, and the two have become inextricably bound together.

Whilst the history of self-organisation goes back a long way (Campbell, 1996), there has been considerable growth of disabled people's and service users' movements since the 1970s (Beresford, 1997). The growth and development of the independent living movement was discussed earlier in the chapter. There are numerous lessons to be learnt from the growth of self-help and user groups. Organisations have usually followed the principles and values of community development by emphasising collective organisation and self-organisation. The concept of community has been based on a 'community of interest' rather than a geographical area, but it nonetheless utilises the principles of community development. Self-advocacy, for example, happens when people speak and act on their own behalf and take a more active role in their own community (Williams and Shoultz, 1982). The emergence of self-advocacy groups such as People First and Survivors Speak Out has been a significant development in recent decades.

People First encourages people with learning difficulties to take control of their own lives. It began in North America and was started in the United Kingdom in the mid 1980s. The organisation has local groups and a national office that supports the development of self-advocacy. Many self-advocacy groups are associated with it. The groups are made up of people with learning difficulties and are often based in training centres, hostels and special schools. The growth of these groups has been influenced by the ideas surrounding normalisation and social role valorisation mentioned previously. Another example of self-advocacy groups is Survivors Speak Out, which provides support for people who have experienced mental distress and associated health problems. They give advice on how to set up and run a self-advocacy group, produce a self-advocacy action pack and provide skilled workers to give assistance and advice in the area where a group wishes to operate.

There are now a number of other national umbrella organisations for user groups and self-help groups, for example the British Council of Organisations of Disabled People and the United Kingdom Advocacy

Network. User organisations played an important part in bringing about the direct payments legislation and the anti-discrimination legislation (Priestley, 1999). The Carers National Association is an umbrella organisation for carers' groups and was an active lobbyist for the Carers (Recognition and Services) Act 1995.

Developments in the self-organisation of users of welfare services illustrate much diversity amongst user groups (Barnes, 1997). The self-help organisations enable previously unconsulted groups to have their voices heard and make their views known. Barnes argues that these organisations are not solely concerned with the redistribution of material goods or with changing the balance of power, 'they are also seeking to change the nature of the discourse within which notions of age, disability and mental disorder are constructed' (ibid., p. 70). Literature on user empowerment and self-help for older people is less in evidence, although there have been some initiatives to give older people a voice in community care (Thornton and Tozer, 1995; Jack, 1995; Cormie, 1999).

■ Community development and community care

Community care takes place within a community context and a useful avenue to explore in this respect is the connection between user involvement and community development. Historically, many users have been segregated from the general population and socially excluded from mainstream society. User empowerment needs to be considered not only in terms of individual empowerment but also from the perspective of collective empowerment, empowerment to relate to the wider community and empowerment as part of the wider community (Barr *et al.*, 1997).

Identifying opportunities for empowerment was made difficult by the intensely individualistic interpretation of community care during the 1990s. Earlier chapters have noted the process whereby a decision is made as to whether a person should receive a comprehensive assessment. If they do then their needs are set against 'eligibility criteria'. Individuals who meet these criteria receive a service. The structures are set up to target individuals in 'greatest need'. In the Department of Health's guidance for practitioners on the community care changes (DoH, 1991b) there was no mention of a community approach. The emphasis was on setting up individual care management with individual assessment, care plans and packages of care. Thus discussions of empowerment frequently just related to 'individual' empowerment and did not consider the other collective aspects. The possibilities provided by such individual 'empowerment' were inevitably narrow and limited.

Techniques and skills of community development can influence these different aspects of empowerment. The philosophy of community development focuses on people who are excluded or oppressed, the structural causes of exclusion or oppression, collective social change, high levels of participation and the process of change. The strategies and skills employed in community development have been drawn on a great deal in health promotion work and there are advocates for them in other areas of health work (Clarke, 1998).

Community development skills have at times been seen as core social work skills (see for example Barclay Report, 1982), but these tended to be lost as a result of the intensely individualistic nature of community care during the 1990s. However a case can still be made for social and health workers to draw on community work skills to empower community care users. An approach that seeks to empower people through collective action would not sit easily with the individualistic orientation of many agencies. There are however possibilities of linking community development and community care through the user-empowerment rhetoric of the community care changes which can be linked to the participatory traditions of community work.

We have seen that the development and growth of self-help groups, user groups and new social movements was one of the most interesting and inspiring aspects of the 1980s and 1990s. This bottom-up growth raises the question of whether community care practitioners can link up with such groups in a way that is constructive and neither patronising nor colonising (that is, the practitioners should not take over). Are there ways in which practitioners can move away from their individualistic orientation towards greater user involvement and a more collective approach? The rhetoric of empowerment and user involvement used by agencies and the Department of Health can be drawn on to develop approaches that are more collective and participatory in nature. There is also much to be learnt from the community social work approaches that flourished in the 1980s (Darvil and Smale, 1990).

Community care workers need new visions of the way things might be. Practitioners who take a wider perspective may be criticised and need valid arguments to justify their practice. The user-empowerment rhetoric of the community care changes provides just such an argument as workers can claim that they are putting official principles into practice.

Barr *et al.* (1997) list the values that community care and community development have in common: empowerment, social inclusion, partnership, needs-led approaches, and participation. They outline four ways in which community development overlaps with user involvement and thus has a role to play in community care:

- *Collective user influence on service provision.* This concerns the level of control and influence users and carers have over the services they use. The emphasis here is on self-advocacy and empowerment. Suggested examples range from community advisory committees to full user control of the service.

- *Collective policy planning influence.* This concerns the influence users and carers have over the policy framework that determines the services they receive. Examples here are the care forums that have been introduced by a number of authorities.
- *Community service provision.* This is service provision by users/carers on their own or by other community organisations.
- *Supportive communities.* The focus here is on changes and developments within neighbourhoods to create more favourable conditions for community care users or carers to become integrated into community life. Examples include good neighbour schemes, volunteering, circles of support and community education.

It is through the user-empowerment aspects of the community care changes that a link can be made to collective empowerment of care users and carers as communities of interest and to the role neighbourhoods can play in supporting community care. There is clearly a gap between rhetoric and reality in respect to user empowerment and community development can help to bridge this gap. Barr *et al.* (ibid., p. 141) present a number of case studies and argue that 'The case studies illustrate that community development is an approach which takes forward user involvement and participation and seeks to make clear links between care user groups and the society of which they are a part'. They urge that a stronger connection be made between community care and community development, saying that health and welfare professionals have embraced the rhetoric of concepts such as empowerment, participation and anti-discriminatory practice but have continued to pursue an individualistic approach to assessment and care planning. 'This myopia constrains the application of these concepts which find their real potential in collective action by and with communities to meet their own needs and pursue more relevant and effective services' (ibid., p. 150).

If community care is to be truly empowering, then it must empower people beyond their role as services users and carers. The aim is that previously marginalised and excluded people should become part of the local community and participate in it (Barnes, 1997). Barnes argues that the concept of community care needs to be widened to include community participation. If this is to be achieved 'It has to involve enabling people to participate in decision making processes about services, and in social, economic and political life more broadly' (ibid., p. 172).

A wider interpretation of community care is needed rather than a narrowing down to individual care packages. With this wider vision it is possible to draw on the real strengths of users/carers to ensure that they make an effective contribution to the well-being of society. Community work approaches give ideas on how this wider vision can be achieved by practitioners. Practitioners of preventive health care are at the front of the field in recognising the importance of community work in achieving a positive change in health at the local level (DoH, 1999b).

■ Models of empowerment

So far this chapter has considered government policy in relation to empowerment and then the influence on practice of the idea of independent living, the social model, normalisation, the user movement and anti-oppressive practice. The practice of community development has also exerted some influence, but it is argued that this could be taken much further.

Most people claim to be in favour of empowerment, but is it simply the case that it is a contested term and different people apply different meanings to it? One way of exploring this is to think in terms of models of empowerment. One such model is that of the consumer who has a greater choice of services. This is called the consumerist model. An alternative model is where the user has greater control over the services and this can be called the democratic model (Beresford and Croft, 1993; Robson *et al.*, 1997).

The consumerist model views users as consumers. Essentially the user has a greater range of services from which to choose. Governments of the 1980s and early 1990s aimed to impose market ideas on public service provision, and consumerism in the public services meant bringing market principles to bear. A key element of the consumerist approach to public services is that the user has more choice because of the greater range of services on offer. The purchaser/provider split is seen as central to this. The user has more and clearer information on the services available and who the services are for. Representation and advocacy may be available for users, although as we have seen this is only in the DoH guidance and not in the legislation itself. There is access to a complaints procedure. In this model these are all key factors in making the services more responsive to users as consumers.

Whilst the consumerist model has been associated with New Right politics and ideas, the democratic model has been associated with the emergence of disabled people's organisations, self-advocacy and service users' organisations and movements (Croft and Beresford, 1999). Central to the democratic model is the idea of users having a greater say in and control over services as well as greater choice. This model draws on traditions of community work and community action, which have always strongly emphasised power and participation issues. The consumerist model emphasises information for users and user involvement but is not really concerned with user power. Customers in a shop can choose between the selection of products on display and have a certain choice between different shops, but they do not determine what is put on the shelf, that is, they have very little power over the selection of products from which to choose.

Consumerism in health and welfare services can be subjected to the same criticism as choice is limited. For example an older person may be able to choose between three day centres, but that is as far as it goes.

Taken further, users could be given a say in whether they want day centres, where the day centres should be located, what goes on in them and how decisions are taken within them. The consumerist model lacks this dimension of power over what is provided and how it is provided.

■ A ladder of empowerment

So far two models of empowerment have been described. In reality it may be more helpful to think in terms of a 'ladder of empowerment' with a succession of steps or stages. In their training pack on community care and community development Barr *et al.* (1997, p. 21) describe the stages shown in Box 7.2.

Box 7.2   A ladder of empowerment

'**Manipulation** – Creating an illusion of participation resulting in disempowerment.
Informing – Telling people what is planned.
Consultation – Offering options and listening to feedback.
Deciding Together – Encouraging others to provide additional ideas and join in deciding the best way forward.
Acting Together – Deciding together and forming partnerships to act.
Supporting Independent Community Interests – Helping others to do what they want.'

Some of the ideas discussed earlier in the chapter can be applied to this ladder. It was noted earlier that disability groups campaigned for many years for direct payments to be made to them so that they could pay for their own care. This sprang from the independent living movement for people with physical disabilities. A similar idea in relation to people with learning difficulties is incorporated into what has become known as 'supported living'. Schemes like this are close to 'supporting independent community interests'. As you move to the other end of the ladder users have less and less control over the services on offer and less and less say in how they are provided.

■ Social exclusion and regeneration

Chapter 1 introduced the notion of social exclusion in relation to community care. It also stressed the need for practitioners to make connections between personal problems and the wider structural issues of, for example, poverty or inadequate housing. This section returns to that theme. In poor areas (or areas particularly identified as in need of regeneration) there are often a large number of community care concerns. This might be because there are high concentrations of people with mental health problems or drug/alcohol problems. Problems that affect whole communities are not best responded to by individualistic responses by health and social care services. During the 1980s and early 1990s the emphasis of regeneration was on economic objectives and the role of the private sector. Regeneration policies and approaches since the mid-1990s however, have clearly included a social dimension (SEU, 1998). These government policies have an important role to play in developing a sensible way forward in community care. Community care workers can help by moving on from 'picking up the pieces' in a poor area to helping the whole community and its people to move forward, improve the quality of their lives and have some say over the future of their area.

Community care's individualising approach is a highly inadequate response and other approaches are required. As Davey (1999) has written, 'People who are seriously disadvantaged in society rarely have single problems – they have multiple interlocking problems . . . . Empowerment must address all their problems together if it is to be meaningful.' A broad approach, tackling the interlocking problems and looking for the common causes, is essential.

Tackling social exclusion has been a major theme of New Labour policies before and since the 1997 election. The Social Exclusion Unit (SEU), set up in December 1997, is based in the Cabinet Office and reports directly to the Prime Minister on how to 'develop integrated and sustainable approaches to the worst housing estates, including crime, drugs, unemployment, community breakdown, and bad schools, etc.' (SEU, 1998). The SEU's remit is confined to England, although similar policies have been adopted in the rest of the UK.

In its early months the SEU was instructed to focus on three areas – truancy, homelessness and neighbourhood renewal, the last two clearly having direct relevance to community care. In relation to homelessness, there was an ambitious target of cutting homelessness by two-thirds by the year 2002. With regard to neighbourhood renewal, the government launched the 'New Deal For Communities', backed by £800 million to tackle problems on England's worst estates. The background and proposals were published in a report by the SEU in 1998. Pilot 'pathway' areas were to be expanded into a 10–20 year plan to turn around deprived neighbourhoods, reduce dependency and empower local communities to shape a better future for themselves.

A problem that many of those involved in regeneration projects have stressed is that the mainstream public services in poor neighbourhoods are frequently ineffective (ibid., p 10). In spite of numerous demands for programmes to be 'bent' towards the needs of poor areas, there is little evidence that this happens (ibid., p. 38). The requirement here is for health and social care agencies to bend their provision towards poor areas and use their resources in an imaginative way. There is a need to analyse the problems, understand what the government is trying to do with area-based projects and work with the policies rather than against them. A key point is that the mainstream welfare services and indeed societal structures can encourage and create exclusion or inclusion. As Parkinson (1998, p. 34) states 'Explicit urban strategies can make a difference, but mainstream programmes make a greater one.' Thus mainstream policies and practices within health and social work need to change. Box 7.3 gives some examples of the ways in which some links have been made between health care and regeneration.

Box 7.3   Examples of links between health care and regeneration

- The Healthy Cities movement has stressed the links between health outcomes and structural problems.
- The Labour government's preventive health care agenda has made links between inequality and health outcomes and the need for health services to tackle these connections (DoH, 1999b).
- Health Action Zones were set up to try to bring more appropriate, better coordinated and more sensitive health services to poor areas.
- A publication by the King's Fund argues powerfully for putting mental health firmly onto the regeneration agenda (Hoggett *et al.*, 1999).
- A Health Education Authority publication called *Putting Health On The Regeneration Agenda* (HEA, 1998) describes the proceedings of a conference on making health issues a more central part of regeneration initiatives.

The SEU report notes the need for the involvement of local people and for community development to be a central part of the regeneration strategy, noting that 'it has become conventional wisdom that communities need to be involved both in designing what is to be done and in implementing it, and that the best policies work through genuine partnerships' (SEU, 1998, p. 34). It is important for workers in mainstream programmes such as community care to back the policies and practices of the local regeneration strategy. It is acknowledged that regeneration requires local participation to be successful, so it follows that community care activities must also be participatory and collective. In reality they are often the very opposite of this. The SEU report stresses the role to be played by local people:

The most powerful resource in turning around neighbourhoods should be the community itself. Community involvement can take many forms: formal volunteering; helping a neighbour; taking part in a community organisation. It can have the triple benefit of getting things done that need to be, fostering community links and building the skills, self-esteem and networks of those who give their time' (ibid., p 68).

These are all ideas to which social workers with a community dimension to their activities should be able to relate strongly (Barclay Report, 1982).

Mutual aid and self-help are seen as crucial to addressing the issues of poverty, exclusion and regeneration (Burns and Taylor, 1998). The Labour government has placed some emphasis on communitarian ideas and mutual aid. Thus community work strategies and skills have much to offer in relation to tackling social exclusion. If community care work is to make a contribution in this area then it needs to break free from the individualistic philosophy of the Thatcher years. Community work has a history of both tackling social divisions and working to empower people (Mayo, 1998).

Regeneration strategies are frequently concerned with issues of direct interest to community care service users. A housing strategy needs to have supported housing as a central part of its agenda. An employment strategy needs to have policies to assist disabled people enter the job market. Hence the importance of community care users and workers being involved directly and closely in the development of local policy.

Social workers and community care workers have an important role to play in fostering social inclusion (Barry and Hallett, 1998) and regeneration. The ideas of exclusion relate very readily to the ideas of anti-oppressive practice. Some views of exclusion have focused on the labour market but a wider definition clearly incorporates exclusion as a result of social divisions such as gender, race, disability and age.

■ Practice issues

As an exercise, if you are a practitioner, reflect on a situation in which you are involved – this could be to do with an individual, a group or the wider community. Try to place that situation on the ladder of user involvement prescribed in Box 7.2. What are some of the blockages to moving to a position of greater user empowerment on the ladder? Can those blockages be removed?

Service users often need information in order to challenge decisions made about them. A range of ways in which decisions on care management can be challenged are given at the end of Chapter 4. Practitioners need to be knowledgeable about these mechanisms in order to provide information at appropriate times.

This chapter has argued that there was more rhetoric than reality about user empowerment in the community care changes. Other changes and influences have, however, encouraged empowerment in different ways and the influence of the independent living movement, the social model of disability, normalisation, the user movement, anti-racist and anti-oppressive practice, and community work has been discussed. All have provided some vision, progress and encouragement when other pressures have forced practice into an individualistic and bureaucratic mode. It has been further argued that Labour policies on social exclusion and regeneration offer opportunities for community care workers to engage in the wider debates and practices (focussing on participation, involvement and change) that are evolving. To avoid this would be to miss the opportunity presented by the Department of Health:

> More widely, social services can make an important contribution to wider local authority-led programmes to tackle the problems of home-lessness, poor housing conditions, and social exclusion in deprived neighbourhoods. These issues, and the need for coordinated local approaches to tackle them, have been covered in the Social Exclusion Unit's reports on rough sleepers and on neighbourhood renewal (DoH, 1998a, para. 6.23).

There is a tendency to see empowerment in purely individual terms. Whilst this is important, this chapter has stressed the desirability of collective empowerment strategies through involvement in self-help groups and community development. Practitioners need to consider how they can acquire skills that are relevant to this and be open to the possibilities it presents. Stewart (1993) argues for much more coverage in nursing education of working in partnership with self-help groups. Health care may too easily fall into the pattern of individual diagnosis and the prescription of drugs in cases where mutual support may be more relevant and helpful.

Practitioners should find out which user groups are operating in their area of work and consider the ways in which support might be given. Care should be taken to act sensitively and to avoid the 'I know best' attitude exhibited by some professional workers. There should be initiatives following on from the Community Care (Direct Payments) Act 1996 that can be supported and helped. This legislation was campaigned for by disabled people's organisations and it needs support if it is to be effectively implemented.

The Labour government has opened up debates and started policy initiatives on tackling exclusion and promoting regeneration. Community care practitioners need to be familiar with these and engage in them as they offer the opportunity to break free from the individualistic interpretation of community care. Primary Care Groups, Health Action Zones and regeneration policy initiatives offer some possibilities.

Priestley (1999) has looked at the Derbyshire Integrated Living Scheme in the context of the wider user movement and national and international policies and developments. Practitioners need to try to make the same connections between local work and wider national and international developments. A quotation from Priestley's book is worth reflecting on in this respect: 'There are many battles to be won and the sheer scale of those which remain requires the maintenance of a visionary agenda for the liberation of disabled people. As the example of disabled people's organisations in Derbyshire shows, acting locally and thinking globally has proved to be good maxim for action' (ibid., p. 226).

☐ *Further reading*

J. Campbell and M. Oliver, *Disability Politics* (London: Routledge, 1996). This book gives a good sense of the growth of disability politics, disability organisations and the way in which disabled people have built up their own movement.

P. Campbell and V. Lindow, *Changing Practice: Mental Health Nursing and User Empowerment* (London: Mind and the Royal College of Nursing, 1997). A useful booklet for nurses and others who work with users of mental health services.

M. Priestley, *Disability Politics and Community Care* (London: Jessica Kingsley, 1999). This book addresses the relationship between the politics of disability and community care policies. The study presents a different vision of community care from that which has resulted from the NHS&CC Act 1990.

N. Thompson, *Promoting Equality* (London: Macmillan, 1998). This book provides a framework for understanding discrimination and oppression. It gives an overview of the literature and discusses what can be learnt from previous experience.

Two books on empowerment that are helpful to practitioners are:

S. Braye and M. Preston-Shoot, *Empowering Practice in Social Care* (Buckingham: Open University Press, 1995).

J. Dalrymple and B. Burke, *Anti-Oppressive Practice: Social Care and the Law* (Buckingham: Open University Press).

☐ *World Wide Web sites*

The British Council of Disabled People was set up in 1981 and is an umbrella organisation representing over 120 disabled people's groups. Its web site is at

http://www.bcodp.org.uk/

This chapter has made connections between empowerment and regeneration policies. A comprehensive regeneration information service is available at

http://www.regen.net

The homepage of the Social Exclusion Unit can be found at

http://www.cabinet-office.gov.uk/seu/

■ *Chapter 8* ■

Adult Abuse and Community Care

Chapter summary
This chapter discusses: • Elder abuse as a developing social problem in the UK. • Some links between adult abuse, child abuse and domestic violence. • Definitions, types and prevalence of abuse. • Institutional abuse. • The legal context of abuse. • Causes of abuse. • Intervention and practice.

■ Introduction

The abuse of adults brings together many of the topics discussed in this book. Interdisciplinary approaches, links to assessment and care management, empowerment, informal carers and networks of care – all these themes of previous chapters are important when considering the abuse of adults.

One of the big omissions in the 1989 White Paper (DoH, 1989a) and the NHS&CC Act 1990 was the subject of adult abuse. Since the 1970s policies and practice in relation to child abuse have been high on the political agenda. The neglected area of domestic violence came to prominence in the 1970s and 1980s, largely as a result of the actions and campaigns of women. The abuse of older people and vulnerable adults has been slower to emerge as an issue of public concern. A year after the community care legislation was passed, Virginia Bottomley (then Junior Minister of Health) stated on television that 'I don't frankly think that abuse of the elderly is a major issue, thank goodness, in our society' ('Newsnight', BBC2, 4 June 1991).

This lack of government acknowledgement of elder abuse helps to explain why it was ignored during the development of legislation and policy for adults. However, the growing evidence of its prevalence and increasing concern about it makes it central to considerations of community care. This chapter starts by exploring the connections between adult abuse, child abuse and domestic violence. There is a particular focus on elder abuse and the development of the issue. This is followed by comment on the definition of abuse, types of abuse, their prevalence and the settings in which they occur. Intervention needs to be grounded in the current legal context and take account of ageism, sexism and disablism, so there is coverage of these and other causes of abuse. The chapter finishes by looking at some ideas on intervention.

■ Adult abuse, child abuse and domestic violence

The topic of abuse is complicated by a plethora of definitional and conceptual differences. What may be considered as abuse by one generation or one society may not be seen as such by another. Both adult abuse and child abuse are socially constructed. How abuse is seen reflects the values and views of a particular time and a particular culture. It is therefore not easy to define, although any one society at any one time may define it for the purposes of intervention and action against it.

There are both similarities and differences between domestic violence, child abuse, elder abuse and the abuse of other vulnerable adults. It is important to search for both those aspects. Child abuse is readily identifiable as an issue of concern or a social problem and has been since the Maria Colwell inquiry of the early 1970s. Domestic violence was largely neglected by the health and welfare services until it was brought to their attention by the women's movement and the refuge movement. The abuse of people with disabilities and with mental health problems has been neglected, and there is little literature, media coverage or research to draw on. Elder abuse has emerged as a social problem since the late 1980s. It can be seen and analysed in terms of the 'development of a social problem' (Penhale and Kingston, 1995, p. 226; Manthorpe, 1999). Box 8.1 picks out some of the key events and research that led to the gradual acknowledgement of elder abuse as a social problem.

Box 8.1 The development of elder abuse in the UK as a social problem

1960s

- Institutional abuse was taken seriously as a result of the writing of people such as Townsend (*The Last Refuge*, 1962) and Robb (*Sans Everything*, 1967).

1970s

- Social worker Mervyn Eastman, using his own records and other contacts and information, drew attention to the issue in the mid 1970s. Journalists and editors gave the unfortunate (and unacceptable) label of 'Granny Bashing' to the phenomenon.

1980s

- The voluntary organisation Age Concern played an important role in keeping the issue on the agenda and in 1984 it published *Old Age Abuse* by Eastman. This was followed in 1986 by *The Law and Vulnerable Elderly People* (Age Concern, 1986), which included coverage of abuse.
- The problem was identified in the UK and North America at about the same time, but while it received attention as a policy and practice issue in the United States, the UK was slow to respond. In the United States, Pillemer and Wolf's *Elder Abuse* (1986) was regarded as a seminal work. The topic maintained a high profile and most US states now have clear legislation in relation to elder abuse.
- In 1988 a British Geriatric Society conference drew together practitioners and stimulated debate. The conference report suggested that 10 per cent of older people were victims of abuse (Bennett *et al.*, 1997, p. 13).

1990s

- The publication of a 1992 study on the prevalence of elder abuse in the UK promoted further debate (Ogg and Bennett, 1992).
- Practice guidance to local authorities, *No Longer Afraid* (DoH, 1993) was published when the authorities were grappling with the implemention of the community care changes. However it was not integral to those changes. No money was allocated to support the guidance and no action was taken against local authorities that failed to heed the guidance. *No Longer Afraid* advocated that care management principles be applied to situations of abuse. Whilst it recommended a strong interagency approach, it was addressed only to social service authorities and not to other statutory bodies such as health authorities (Ambache, 1997).
- A number of other works (many of which are mentioned in this chapter) published in the 1990s helped to raised the profile of the issue.
- The organisation Action on Elder Abuse was formed in 1993 and has since played an important role in breaking the taboo on examining and discussing the issue. It set up a national telephone helpline in 1997.
- A campaign by *Community Care* magazine in 1993 highlighted the issue for social work practitioners.
- Consultation papers by the English Law Commission and the Scottish Law Commission on vulnerable adults were published during the early 1990s and these triggered debate on the weakness of legislation in this area.
- At the local level, most social service authorities drew up and adopted policies and procedures relating to elder abuse during the 1990s, usually in consultation with other agencies such as health authorities. These documents provide valuable guidelines for practitioners. However these policies varied from area to area so there has been uneven development. There remains a need for a national strategy and a national lead.
- In December 1997 the government published a Green Paper, 'Who Decides?' (Lord Chancellor's Department, 1997), containing the package of proposals relating to England and Wales that had been put together by the Law Commission in 1995. Among the proposals were the modernisation of laws relating to mental incapacity, and the introduction of new powers to enable social workers to intervene to protect vulnerable adults such as elderly people, those with serious physical illnesses and those incapable of making their own decisions.

> • In 1998 the 'Practitioner Alliance Against Abuse of Vulnerable Adults' was set up in order to bring practitioners together and give them a voice in the ongoing debate.

Since the 1970s in the UK there has been considerable publicity about and reports, legislation and research on child abuse, from which it may be possible to draw some lessons that are applicable to elder abuse. In child protection there are a range of orders under the Children Act 1989 (in Scotland the Children (Scotland) Act 1995) that can be called on. These include emergency protection orders and child assessment orders, posing the question as to whether similar orders might be appropriate in the case of vulnerable adults.

It is easy to focus on the lack of legislation and procedures for adults in contrast with the numerous measures to protect children and to assume automatically that similar legislation would be helpful. Whilst it is important to learn from experiences in the field of child abuse, there needs to be an awareness of some of the issues and problems of the child protection system itself (DoH, 1995c). For example child protection registers are part of the machinery, as are child protection conferences. If there is to be good interprofessional working in relation to adult abuse there has to be a sharing of information. This sharing has to be done sensibly and properly, which suggests the need for some kind of list or register. However child care workers' experience of such registers has not been entirely positive and there is evidence of considerable variation in the use of registers throughout the country (ibid., p. 31). Also, the registration and conferencing systems have resulted in a large number of resources going to protect a small number of children, while many other children in need receive very little help (ibid., p. 55). There are lessons to be learnt from these experiences in relation to adults.

Social work in child care has become dominated by child protection work and Eastman (1999) poses the question of whether social work with adults would become dominated by investigative work if there was a stronger legal framework. If resources were tight, would other aspects of social work with adults become neglected? Eastman therefore argues that there may be a case for leaving the police to deal with this investigative work.

Good interprofessional working in child protection has been helped and fostered by 'area child protection committees'. There may be a case for similar bodies in the field of adult/elder abuse, and indeed some have already been set up. There has been an emphasis on 'procedures' in child protection. This has also been taking place in relation to adult/elder abuse, with many authorities writing procedural policies. On the other hand one has to ask whether models developed specifically for children are appropriate for adults.

There is a wealth of experience in child protection work on 'disclosure', with some obvious lessons to learn. With both groups this work requires skill and sensitivity. Disclosure can happen at any time, for example at a day centre or alone with a home care worker. It is essential for all workers to have some idea of how to respond. No worker can promise confidentiality in this situation and they need to make it clear that they are obliged to inform their line manager. Again there may be lessons from child protection practice of the best way to investigate a situation, and of the most satisfactory organisation and format of case conferences. One possible lesson that has emerged from child protection is the necessity to avoid over zealousness. There may be no substance to a disclosure, or alternatively, adults may choose not to talk about the issue. Such situations can provoke anxiety in workers and lead to the undue pressurising of service users.

In relation to domestic violence, there is a need to see victims of domestic violence within the wider context of community care and to investigate any possible links between domestic violence and other abuse of adults. What should be the same and what different in respect of policies, procedures and intervention? Some elder abuse is the continuation of abuse from earlier years and yet relatively few links have been made between the two areas of study. As McCreadie (1996, p.17) writes, 'the domestic violence literature has barely concerned itself with older people and the elder abuse literature has barely concerned itself with domestic violence'.

Connections are now being made and a useful book by Kingston and Penhale (1995) draws out some of these connections. Biggs *et al.* (1995, p. 110) argue that domestic violence intervention models tend to stress crisis intervention services, emergency refuges, support groups, counselling facilities and legal expertise. The emphasis is on providing immediate protection once the abuse is identified. This contrasts with the approach to other forms of adult abuse, where there has often been a reluctance to act. Police forces have been increasingly encouraged to treat domestic abuse as a crime but this is less the case in other areas of adult abuse.

It should be clear that abuse is not a straightforward problem for which there are easy answers or solutions. It is far easier to provide a list of questions on the topic that are largely unresolved. Box 8.2 lists some of these.

Box 8.2   Questions for debate

- Should child abuse, domestic abuse and adult abuse be considered as similar or different phenomena?
- If abuse can occur throughout the life cycle, what is the justification for categorisation by age? (Slater, 1999)
- Are there common roots, explanations and interventions, or should we be cautious of drawing such links?

- Should neglect be considered as abuse, and if so what is the limitation on the individual liberty to choose to live as they wish?
- At what point does verbal aggression become psychological abuse?
- Why are there police checks on people working with children but not on people working with vulnerable adults?
- Should there be an 'at risk' register for abused adults?
- Abuse also takes place outside the domestic sphere, so how do we consider abuse within institutional or community settings?
- Why is the criminal justice system so insensitive to the needs of vulnerable adults?
- Should the lead workers investigating the abuse of adults be social workers or the police? (Eastman, 1999)

It is clear that there are many questions and most of them stimulate debate rather than answers.

■ Definition, types of abuse and prevalence

There are a number of definitions of abuse in current use. After discussion and consultation the group, Action on Elder Abuse produced the following definition: 'Elder abuse is a single or repeated act or lack of appropriate action occurring within any relationship where there is an expectation of trust which causes harm or distress to an older person.' An alternative approach is to locate elder abuse within the category of abuse of vulnerable adults. For example in 1991 Leeds Social Services made the following definition: 'The physical, psychological, sexual or financial abuse or neglect of a vulnerable adult by a person or persons who regularly exercise powers to violate the human and civil rights of that adult. The abuse may be active (acts of commission) or passive (acts of omission)' (McCreadie, 1996, p. 9). Social service authorities have increasingly moved towards policies that apply to all vulnerable adults rather than just older people.

It is hard to determine the extent of abuse as it depends on what is defined as abuse. For example do we include financial and emotional abuse and what sort of behaviour do we include within this? Whilst the debate goes on there is widespread agreement about five main categories of abuse: physical, psychological or emotional, financial, sexual, and neglect. Abuse can take place in numerous settings, such as a person's own home, a carer's home, a residential home, a nursing home, a day care setting or a hospital.

Abuse is bound to be hidden to a large extent because it is not something that people readily talk about. According to the Social Services Inspectorate, in 1993 'the scale of the problem is not known nor whether it is on the increase. There is no accepted way of recording reported cases, let alone unreported or undetected cases' (DoH, 1993, p. 3). Abuse is a complex phenomenon. It takes different forms, occurs in different settings and takes place in various kinds of relationship.

The first indication of the scale of the problem in the UK was provided by Ogg and Bennett (1992), who reported on the results of structured interviews with 593 people aged 65 and over. Excluded were older people in institutions and those who were too ill or disabled to participate, and this may have concealed the true extent of abuse. Fifty people reported some kind of abuse. Of these nine reported physical abuse, nine financial abuse and 32 verbal abuse. Adult members of households in regular contact with a person of pensionable age were asked if they had ever abused an older person. Of the 1366 questioned, 10 per cent admitted to verbal abuse and 1 per cent acknowledged physical abuse (ibid.). Whilst limited in nature, this study did demonstrate that there was a serious problem.

Whilst elder abuse has been neglected the abuse of other vulnerable adults has received even less attention. Little is known, for example, about the abuse of people with mental health problems. It is of course hard to obtain reliable figures as abuse is shrouded in secrecy. With regard to people with learning difficulties, in a study by Brown and colleagues at the University of Kent in the early 1990s it is estimated that at that time there were around 1200 new cases each year of the sexual abuse of adults with learning difficulties in England and Wales (Craft, 1996). The lesson here for practitioners is that they should be alert to the possibility that it is taking place.

Some older people and other vulnerable adults suffer harassment from strangers in the community. 'Community harassment' or 'stranger abuse' is little researched, but in some city areas older people are afraid to leave their houses and some individuals have suffered considerable abuse and persecution (Biggs *et al.*, 1995, p. 74). Pritchard (1995, p. 32) has written of the growing concern about older people being abused by young people in their communities, and of the growing problem of drug abuse in the UK and the link between this and the abuse of elders. With black adults there can also be an element of racism in abuse (Biggs, 1996). Individualised care management is an inappropriate response to this community problem and there is a need, as stressed in Chapter 7, for links to neighbourhood regeneration policies and policies that deal with discrimination and social exclusion.

■ Institutional abuse

The 1993 DoH guidelines concentrated on abuse in the home. This was rather strange given that scandals about abuse in institutions go back some decades. The practice of care in the community was given particular impetus by the abuse, neglect and shameful conditions revealed by a succession of hospital inquiries (concerning people with learning difficulties and mental health problems). Earlier examples include Ely in 1968, South Ockenden in 1969, Farleigh in 1970 and Whittingham in 1971. Further inquiries took place in the late 1970s, including the one into Normansfield Hospital in 1978.

Given this history, it is important to consider institutional settings, such as day care facilities, residential homes, nursing homes and hospitals (Clough, 1996). People often enter these settings so that they can be cared for and kept safe, but sadly they may still find themselves victims of abuse. Concern about institutional abuse has played a part in the move towards community care. As McCreadie (1996, p. 57) writes, 'As numerous enquiries into grave deficiencies in various areas of institutional care for all age groups have shown, abuse flourishes within a culture which allows it to be acceptable'. Pritchard (1996, pp. 114–15) notes that abuse can be perpetuated by a member of staff against a resident, a resident against a member of staff, a resident against another resident or an outsider against a resident. This can take place in any institutional setting. Section 48 of the NHS&CC Act 1990 required the setting up of Inspection Units within social service authorities to inspect all residential homes for adults.

The local authority Registration and Inspection Units and the health authority Inspection Units were part of the official machinery to safeguard against abuse in residential and nursing care. These units were required to inspect all institutions twice a year: one announced inspection and one unannounced. The Labour government announced that these would be replaced by a Commission for Care Standards, which would regulate a wider range of care services and work to national standards. In Scotland there would be a Commission for the Regulation of Care, accountable to the Scottish Parliament, and in Wales a Commission for Care Standards.

Inspections are static snapshots taken at certain times and need to be part of a broader, continuous strategy. Such a strategy would include helping residents to voice their complaints. It would also encourage staff to bring problems into the open without fear of victimisation. The example in Box 8.3 illustrates the difficulty of this.

Box 8.3   Case study

In February 1997 the owner of an old people's home in Yorkshire was jailed for four years after pleading guilty to sexually assaulting women in his care who were suffering from senile dementia. The deputy matron, Judy Jones, risked her job to stop the owner forcing oral sex on elderly residents. She felt unable to raise the matter with the owner's wife, who ran the home, and she knew that if she went to the police it would simply be her word against his. With the help of the charity Public Concern at Work she developed a plan with other staff to protect the residents and obtain the necessary proof.

Public Concern at Work is a charity set up in 1994 which aims to help employees expose serious malpractice in their workplace. A significant proportion of their work has been concerned with abuse in residential and nursing homes. It has a mission to ensure that concerns about serious malpractice are properly raised and addressed. It has called for legal protection for care home staff who expose abuse; a regulatory regime that actively encourages good practice in the sector; and for care homes to operate an open door policy for relatives and friends and to hold open days for the local community. What is needed is a system that enables concerns to be expressed and examined without victimisation. In a way this can be seen as building whistle-blowing into the system as a last resort. The Public Interest Disclosure Act 1998 goes some way towards providing legal protection for whistleblowers.

If institutions are to be safe it is essential for them to remain open to ideas and inspections. When they become 'closed' abuse can become the norm. It is all too easy within a closed society for poor practice to deteriorate into unacceptable conduct. Lawson (1999) powerfully describes how as a trainee nurse in a hospital she felt she was being 'trained' into abusing patients by the experienced nurses with whom she worked. It was only some time later that she recognised that such practices were abusive. In an important and illuminating article drawing on public inquiries into institutional care, Wardhaugh and Wilding (1993) consider how institutions, organisations and staff who are supposedly committed to an ethic of care become 'corrupted' and abuse both their power and people in their care. They discuss how care becomes corrupted and how it can break down so that residents of institutions are put at risk. In order to avoid this 'corruption of care' there need to be built-in safety mechanisms to prevent poor practice from taking hold. This involves a culture of openness, self-criticism, self-regulation, peer criticism, managerial support, supervision and control. What is required is a structure and environment where disclosure can take place naturally and where there are clear policies and procedures that make it easy to raise issues of concern, including abuse. Where mechanisms are in place there should be no need for whistle-blowing, but as a fall-back it would be useful to have procedures for whistle-blowing.

■ The legal context of abuse

Many feel that the national practice guidelines on the abuse of older people are insufficient in themselves and there is a need for a change in the law. There is no clear legal framework for workers to intervene unless a person is 'mentally disordered'. Without the law on their side professional workers are limited in what they can do. The carer can refuse to let professionals have access. The adult victim may refuse help.

Practitioners should bear in mind that there are laws against such crimes as assault, theft and rape and that these laws can be drawn on. There can however be some difficulties with making use of criminal law. The victim of abuse normally has to complain and be involved in the preparation of charges by the police. This can be distressing if a family member is involved. Furthermore the police may be reluctant to pursue cases involving family disputes. There is also a problem with older people and people with disabilities being taken seriously as victims of crime. The Crown Prosecution Service (CPS) has to be satisfied that the prospect of a conviction is good and that it is in the public interest to bring a prosecution. It may, for example, feel that it is not worth wasting public money on someone whom they consider will not perform well in court. Once this obstacle has been passed the court itself has to be convinced. Giving evidence in court can be very stressful for fragile or vulnerable people (Brammer, 1996, p. 40). The process requires oral evidence and often involves heavy cross-examination. In recent years some concessions have been made to children in court situations. Children can give evidence on video tape, and be cross-examined out of the courtroom by means of closed-circuit television. These concessions are not available to adults, no matter how vulnerable they are. Hence there are a number of hurdles and problems in using the criminal justice system to counter abuse, and there has been a groundswell of awareness that access to justice is not equal (Craft, 1996).

There is evidence that people with learning difficulties are seriously disadvantaged by the justice system. This is linked to the negative evaluation of and discrimination against people with learning difficulties by society at large. Researchers at the from Oxford Centre for Criminological Research have looked at the problems that people with learning difficulties can encounter when negotiating the criminal justice system (Sanders *et al.*, 1997). Seventy-six incidents involving people with learning difficulties were studied. Although most of the cases had been reported to the police, less than half had resulted in prosecution, and most of these had ended in acquittal. The study found that criminal justice personnel had little understanding of learning difficulties or their implications. Included in the recommendations were the following:

- Relevant training for the police, crown prosecutors, barristers and judges (see Box 8.4 below as an example).
- Measures to enable people with learning difficulties to give evidence, for example the use of screens, television links and video evidence.
- Pretrial procedures to prepare people for their appearance in the courtroom.
- Greater sensitivity towards people with learning difficulties who are alleged to have committed a crime.

An interdepartmental working group also advocated these and other reforms (Home Office, 1998). It recommended a range of measures in

England and Wales to assist vulnerable and intimidated witnesses to give their best evidence in court.

Box 8.4 Case study

In September 1997 a judge dismissed a case against a care worker charged with indecently assaulting a disabled woman, Mary Nevin, on the ground that the latter was not a competent witness. Mary Nevin could not speak due to multiple sclerosis. She had made her statement to the police with the help of an alphabet board and the process had been recorded on video. The judge refused to let the video-taped material be admitted as evidence. Mary Nevin's request to answer cross-examination questions with an alphabet board was also refused by the judge. Therefore Nevin was prevented from giving evidence and the care worker was acquitted.

(Reported in *Community Care*, 28.8. 97)

These unacceptable aspects of the criminal justice system should be changed. Equally, there is a need for practitioners to tackle any negative attitudes they themselves may have. They may, for example, make ageist or disablist assumptions about what older people or disabled people are capable of withstanding in the pursuit of legal remedies. According to Bennett *et al.* (1997, p. 121), 'Practitioners need to develop methods of enabling older people to withstand the possible rigours of court appearances and assisting them to do so.'

With regard to intervention, it is important for practitioners to be well-informed about current legislation. Obtaining appropriate advice at the correct time from solicitors, law centres, specialist legal departments or charities is an important part of the process. Practitioners should be familiar with the relevant laws and how they might be used so that they can give knowledgeable advice when required. It is important to be able to draw on the law appropriately and at the correct time. Brammer (1996, p. 13) states that 'The challenge of elder abuse . . . calls on lawyers to be creative and use their imagination and skills in drawing on existing remedies from statute and common law and adapting these to respond to individual complaints of elder abuse.'

In the early 1990s the English Law Commission engaged in a process of consultation on the need for changes to the law in respect of mental disability. One consultation paper was published in 1991 and three were published in 1993. The conclusions and recommendations were brought together in a fifth report, *Mental Incapacity* (Law Commission, 1995). This included a draft Mental Incapacity Bill. The original terms of reference were extended to other people who were vulnerable and in need of protection. The report is quite clear that reform is needed: 'The law as it now stands is unsystematic and full of glaring gaps. It does not rest on clear or modern foundations of principle. It has failed to keep up with developments in our understanding of the rights and needs of those with mental disability' (ibid., para. 1.1). Drawing on the Children Act 1989 and models for child protection, the proposals set out a clear framework for the investigation and assessment of situations of abuse (Brammer, 1996, p. 43). The Scottish Law Commission also reviewed the law in this area and published a report in 1995. The underlying principles of the Scottish approach were broadly similar to those of the English Law Commission (Lord Chancellor's Department, 1997).

The main recommendations of the English Law Commission were included in the Green Paper 'Who Decides? (ibid.) One recommendation was that social service authorities should have a new duty to investigate suspected neglect or abuse and be given the power to deal with the protection of people they believe to be at risk. However, at the time of writing it seems that the government has decided not to introduce new legislation but to publish guidance during 2000. In this guidance social service authorities will be expected to take a lead role in coordinating the development of local policy and practice guidance for the protection of vulnerable adults at risk of abuse.

■ Looking for causes

Most accounts of the causes of abuse have concentrated on the stress on carers and on family violence within dysfunctional families. Causes are always complex with many factors involved, but it is noticeable how much of the discussion on adult abuse has ignored wider societal issues. Causes are often described in a localised or narrow way and fail to acknowledge the wider structural issues at play. It is important to bring social divisions to the forefront of discussion and put adult abuse into the context of an ageist, sexist and disablist society. Feminists and feminist theory have placed domestic violence in the context of male power and patriarchal attitudes and structures. Just as racism provides an explanatory backcloth to violence against black people (or heterosexism to violence against gay people) so one needs to see ageism, sexism and disablism as providing an explanatory backcloth to the harm and violence to older people (predominantly women) and disabled people in society (Biggs, 1996).

Theories on carer stress and dysfunctional families have been very much to the fore. Most of the research on the causes of elder abuse has been conducted in the United States. McCreadie (1994, p. 16) summarises the two broad approaches as a function of firstly caregiving and secondly as an aspect of family violence. Similarly, whilst the SSI guidelines acknowledge that there are likely to be many different reasons why older people are abused, it is clear where the emphasis is: 'Carers under stress, or ill-equipped for the caring role, and carers who have been (and are still being) abused themselves, account for a proportion of cases. A history of poor family relationships is a reason for others. In some families the power once exercised by the parent is also probably a factor' (DoH, 1993, p. 4). These guidelines, like most of the literature on abuse, ignore the fact that abuse and harm take place within an ageist, sexist and disablist society and fail to make connections with these structural factors of social division.

Ageism, for example, has a very considerable impact on how old people are viewed and treated (Thompson, 1995). Butler defines it as 'A process of systematic stereotyping and discrimination against people because they are old, just as racism and sexism accomplish this for skin colour and gender' (Butler, 1987, p. 22). This stereotyping and discrimination influences people's attitudes and behaviour. It can reduce the barriers to acts of abuse (Thompson, 1995). Ageism in health and social care organisations may mean that older people receive a worse service than they should receive. It may mean that acts of abuse are not taken as seriously as they would be if the person were younger.

Explanatory frameworks are important because they influence how practitioners see issues and what needs to be done. 'Carer stress' is probably viewed as the 'common sense' explanation of elder abuse. As the older person becomes more dependent he or she makes more demands on the carer. The carer can no longer cope with these demands, resulting in abuse or neglect. This fits into the 'situational stress' theory (Penhale and Kingston, 1995, p. 192). If we accept this explanation then intervention will probably consist of relieving carer stress through some combination of respite service, day care and home care. However such solutions tend to define the victim of abuse as the problem.

Much analysis of domestic violence looks to explanations connected to the power of men in society and within families. Violence is at the end of a continuum that maintains and asserts that power. Such an explanatory framework deriving from feminist writers, leads to theories of intervention that focus on escaping from the situation, removing the offender, and using the law to deal with the crime and protect the woman.

Whittaker (1995, p. 44) states 'Elder abuse, like other forms of abuse, must be seen as a crime against the person'. It is not satisfactory to try to explain it away compassionately as carer stress or the symptom of a dysfunctional family (DoH, 1993). It may be these things but it also a crime and it needs to be seen within the context of male violence to women within families and society (Dobash and Dobash, 1992). It should be located within the patriarchal family rather than the pathological family and it is important to avoid viewing the victim as the problem (Whittaker, 1995; Aitken and Griffin, 1996).

■ Intervention and practice issues

Confronted by a situation of possible adult abuse, practitioners sometimes feel inadequately prepared to cope. This is now less of a reason for inaction as there are guidelines, a body of knowledge and experienced practitioners who can give advice.

The profile of work with older people and disabled people needs to be raised. It is important and skilled work. One of the key issues is to break the taboo on discussing abuse. Denial of it results in people and workers not recognising its existence or not addressing it. It is difficult to deal with and it is sometimes easier to deny what is in front of our eyes. The taboo needs to be broken at all levels because it is one of the factors that inhibits the disclosure of abuse by those abused, their relatives and health and social care workers.

Working in situations of abuse requires considerable skill. It is also potentially very stressful, and as with any really difficult situation it can produce in workers a range of emotions, such as helplessness, fear, blame, guilt, frustration, anger, denial and shame. There will be feelings of 'What could I have done?' or 'What should I have done next?' Thus supervision and support are as important in this area of work as in others. This can help alleviate anxiety and assist in the consideration of all options. It has been pointed out that intervention is influenced by the worker's view of the causes of elder abuse. Much of what has been covered in this book is important to the style of intervention adopted, as indicated below.

Firstly, it is of central importance to develop interdisciplinary strategies and approaches. Abuse situations almost always involve workers from different professions and good interdisciplinary working, as discussed in Chapter 5, is essential.

Secondly, a characteristic of families in which abuse takes place is social isolation. This may be important in terms of risk assessment in that 'older people in isolated kin networks may be more at risk than older people involved in a network where there are a range of people – relatives, friends and neighbours – with whom they interact' (Biggs *et al.*, 1995, p.106; see also Chapter 6 of this book). Identifying and strengthening natural helping networks may be appropriate in some situations.

Thirdly, abuse can be seen as resulting from a lack of power. An advocacy and empowerment approach emphasises the importance of restoring power, with the emphasis on self-determination (Nahmiash, 1999); empowerment was covered in Chapter 7 of this book. Croft and Beresford (1999) have argued cogently that the most effective way to challenge elder abuse is to increase older people's say and involvement in all situations where they are cared for, and indeed in society in general. Linked to this is the argument presented in this chapter that elder abuse needs to be seen in the context of an ageist and sexist society. Anti-ageist and antisexist policies need to be part of intervention strategies in order to change the attitudes that sustain abuse.

Fourthly, in the section on law earlier in the chapter it was indicated that there are a number of laws that can be drawn on. Whilst there may well be a need for new legislation, some would argue that the existing laws could be used much more effectively.

Finally there is the question of assessment. A case of abuse normally requires a comprehensive assessment under the NHS&CC Act 1990. Whilst the Act covers assessment of need there is no mention of what to do if someone is being abused. Furthermore there is no coverage of the investigation of abuse. The 1993 SSI guidelines stressed how they were compatible with the principles of sound assessment and care management and that they should be incorporated within these procedures. 'Agencies should consider how they will ensure that this area of work is effectively handled within the context of their procedures for care management and assessment' (DoH, 1993, p. 9). Stevenson (1996, p. 22) also argues that 'an approach to elder protection which incorporates concern about abuse into a wider framework of need assessment and care management would seem highly desirable'.

McCreadie (1996) argues that Section 47 of the NHS&CC Act 1990 is particularly important in relation to abuse in people's own homes. 'It requires no test of capacity and in focusing on the need for services, and not only social care services, but also health and housing provision, the statute enables workers to address the needs of both parties in the abusive relationship in a wide variety of ways. It is now supported by the 1995 Carers (Recognition and Services) Act' (ibid., p. 93).

In the United States many of the assessment forms and processes take the possibility of abuse into account (Baumhover and Beall, 1996), but this is rarely the case in the UK. However most authorities now have guidelines and procedures relating to elder and/or adult abuse and it is obviously essential for worker to be familiar with these. In their everyday activities health and social care workers should be sensitive to signs and indications of abuse. They need to develop the skill of asking appropriate questions that assist people to talk about abuse. 'Professionals must become comfortable asking questions that encourage elderly people to report abusive behaviour' (ibid., p. 110). McCreadie (1996, p. 93) argues that 'it may be useful to include questions about the risk of abuse in all community care assessments. The SSI (1995) recommend that priority eligibility criteria for an assessment of need should include vulnerability to abuse.'

However McCreadie also stresses that assessment needs time:

> The evidence about elder abuse suggests that many cases, particularly those involving physical and psychological abuse, or multiple abuse, will have behind them human relationships of particular complexity involving dependencies and pathologies. Therefore an assessment needs to examine the history and nature of relationships within the household, as well as the characteristics of both abuser and abused (ibid., p. 95).

An older person may acknowledge the existence of abuse to any worker at any time, but it is more likely to be admitted to someone who has built up a relationship of trust with that person, such as a home care or day centre worker. It is vital that the older person is listened to by that trusted worker and that what she or he says is taken seriously. A common reaction to abuse is denial (Pritchard, 1995, p. 44) and this is one of the reasons why building up trust is a key element of working with people who have been abused. Pritchard writes, 'I believe very strongly that it can take anything between two and four years to get a disclosure about abuse which has been going on for a long time. It is rare that disclosure comes within days, weeks or months of working with a victim' (ibid., p. 47).

Intervention has to be based on sound assessment and it is clear that there are many different situations in which abuse occurs. There are different types of abuse in different types of situation and intervention will differ according to this. In any one society there may well be different perspectives on abuse and neglect. For example black and ethnic minority groups may have differing perspectives. There is little literature and research on this, but a working paper has been published by Action On Elder Abuse (Scott, 1999) and the *Journal of Elder Abuse and Neglect* published a special issue on the topic in 1997 (vol. 9, no. 2). The latter included an article on abuse in respect of gay and lesbian people (Cook-Daniels, 1997). It may be, for example, that people who have a suffered a history of oppression and discrimination find it even more difficult to talk to outside practitioners about abuse within their family and their community.

To conclude, this chapter has stressed how work in the area of adult abuse needs to draw on many of the topics in this book, such as interdisciplinary working, considering social networks, conducting thorough assessments and working in an empowering way. The chapter has stressed that a body of expertise now exists and that most local authorities have guidelines for practitioners. The Kent guidelines are printed at the back of Pritchard's (1995) book. Berkshire's interagency policy on vulnerable adults is included as an appendix in Pritchard (1999). If you are practising as a health or social care worker the first step is to familiarise yourself with the guidelines for your area. Abuse and harm thrive on secrecy and they remain something of a taboo subject. Breaking the taboo helps to break the secrecy, so this is a matter for practitioners to learn about, discuss and address in the workplace and the community. Finally, it is necessary to avoid treating adult abuse as simply an individual concern in a domestic setting. It should be set in a community context and in the national context of discrimination and oppression.

☐ Further reading

P. Kingston and B. Penhale (eds), *Family Violence and the Caring Professions* (London: Macmillan, 1995). This book looks at child abuse, domestic violence and elder abuse. It discusses three groups of people who are subject to abuse, and some of the differences and similarities between issues and interventions are usefully drawn out.

There are a number of helpful 'overview' books. Amongst these are:

G. Bennett, P. Kingston and P. Penhale, *The Dimensions of Elder Abuse* (London: Macmillan, 1997).
S. Biggs, C. Phillipson and P. Kingston (eds), *Elder Abuse in Perspective.* (Buckingham: Open University Press, 1995).
P. Decalmer and F. Glendenning (eds), *The Mistreatment of Elderly People*, 2nd edn (London: Sage, 1997).

The organisation Action on Elder Abuse has a number of publications and leaflets that are useful for practitioners (including one on elder abuse and the law in Scotland). They can be contacted at Action on Elder Abuse, Astral House, 1268 London Road, London, SW 16 4ER.

☐ *World Wide Web sites*

Action on Elder Abuse has a website with information on the organisation itself and adult abuse:

http://www.elderabuse.org

The Practitioner Alliance Against Abuse of Vulnerable Adults has a web site at

http://www.pava.org.uk

The Domestic Violence Data Source is a website for all those with an interest in domestic violence:

http://www.domesticviolencedata.org

Conclusion

This book has discussed some essential issues in community care for health and social care practitioners. It has focused on carers, the shifting boundaries of community care, care management and assessment, interprofessional working, social support, empowerment, and abuse. Practitioners need to have a sound background knowledge of these topics if they are to develop good, reflective practice. This book has endeavoured to provide this and to make these 'essentials' relevant and comprehensible for community care practitioners.

In addition to the topics listed at the start of each chapter, other themes have run throughout the book. This conclusion will summarise these and make some brief comments on developments at the time of writing (Autumn, 1999).

Firstly, it is necessary to bring the community back into community care. Many of the developments during the 1990s were individualising: assessments, care management, care packages and eligibility criteria all focused on the individual. The book has balanced this by emphasising collectivities of carers and users in a community context.

Secondly, and this is linked to the previous point, individual problems need to be understood within wider societal structures. Poverty and social divisions such as race, class, gender, age, sexual orientation and disability are key variables in determining people's experiences of community care. Practice needs to be seen within the context of these divisions and inequalities. Anti-oppressive practice has developed in relation to these structural inequalities. In terms of government policy, since 1997 there has been some movement away from the narrow New Right philosophy of the 1980s and early 1990s, which stressed an individualistic orientation, family care and the development of markets in health and social care.

Thirdly, there is a need to draw on the strengths of both the formal and the informal sector in order to advance community care. The theme of 'interweaving' ran through Chapters 2, 4, 5 and 6 in particular. Practitioners should be able to work effectively with carers and with workers from other agencies and disciplines.

Fourthly, the 'care' within community care has a 'control' dimension. Chapter 5 noted how this can be true for those people with mental health problems who may be a danger to themselves or others. Chapter 8 discussed the complex issue of adult abuse and the need for a variety of strategies to deal with the problem.

Fifthly, the matter of 'shifting boundaries' was introduced in Chapter 3. Community care is rife with boundary, demarcation and funding disputes. This is partially responsible for the 'maze' that the community care system can appear to be to service users.

Sixthly, empowerment was a particular theme of Chapter 7 but it also figured in several other chapters. It has been stressed however that real 'democratic' empowerment is difficult to attain.

Finally, the book has discussed some of the contradictions experienced by practitioners in the community care system. Chapter 4 indicated how practitioners may be expected, for example, to undertake individual needs-led assessments in the face of tight resource constraints. This problem is exacerbated by the fact that they are also expected to promote empowerment, anti-oppressive practice and user involvement. There are real contradictions here. The book has tried to make these contradictions more explicit so that practitioners can be aware of the situation they are in and maximise the possibility of constructive change. By making the contradictions explicit, it becomes possible to identify the issues and reflect on a possible way forward. There is a danger of resolving the contradictory expectations by neglecting the real interests of service users. One possibility is to use some of the current rhetoric and guidance on empowerment to try to work out strategies to meet the needs of service users.

After its election in 1997 the Labour government did not set out to restructure the community care system it had inherited. Rather it aimed to improve and modernise it (DoH, 1998a), and it has energetically published documents and taken initiatives to this end. There has been a very strong push towards interprofessional working and the bringing down of the 'Berlin Wall' between health and social care. It will be interesting to observe and evaluate these changes.

The Royal Commission on Long Term Care reported its findings in early 1999 and its main recommendations were covered in Chapter 3. At the time of writing the government has yet to respond to the proposals. Of central importance to future community care, long-term care is one of the most important social policy issues at the start of the new millennium.

Some significant reforms are under way in the area of health. The formation of Primary Health Groups/Trusts (and their equivalent in Scotland, Wales and Northern Ireland) represent a big change in the way health services are organised and funded. As they move towards 'trust' status they will become major providers and commissioners of health care. One possible future scenario is that they could be the point of contact where the process of community care assessment is arranged and the necessary care commissioned. Community care could be organised in the future under Primary Care Trusts, with social care budgets becoming part of the structure.

Certainly there is a growing consensus about the need for greater integration of community care services. We have seen throughout the book how boundary, demarcation and funding disputes are part of the current picture. In an interesting development the Scottish Office is funding a £1 million project to integrate community care services across social work and health in Perth and Kinross over a three-year period. The objective is to achieve pooled budgets, the single management of all budgets and a joint information technology system, with equal access to the records of all service users (*Community Care*, 5–11 August 1999). Similarly Sterling Council plans to integrate the community care services within the health services over three years (*Community Care*, 26 August–1 September 1999).

April 1999 saw the setting up of the Welsh Assembly and the Scottish Parliament. Health services had previously been run by the Scottish Office and Welsh Office so there already existed a considerable amount of administrative devolution, and this was then taken further with the new national devolution arrangements. The latter may well result in some separate developments in social care and health care provision, leading to variations in community care provision between the different parts of the UK, as illustrated by the two examples from Scotland in the previous paragraph.

The Labour government has introduced policy initiatives in a whole range of areas with relevance to community care practitioners, including an emphasis on urban regeneration, combatting social exclusion and improving public health. These all have links to community care and it has been argued that some of these policies can enable practitioners to break free from the very individualising vision of community care that prevailed in the early and mid-1990s. Thus links can be made in theory and in practice between, for example, community care and social exclusion, community care and health promotion, and community care and participation.

In many ways it is an exciting time to be a practitioner in community care. The growth of the self-help and user movements has been inspiring. There has been a shift towards the social model of disability and the ideas promoted by the independent living movement. New technology is opening further possibilities for people to live comfortably and securely in the community (RCLTC, 1999). The 1997 Labour government brought with it new energy and new initiatives. However the way forward on some issues, for example adult abuse and long-term care, is not yet clear and the debate continues. Practitioners and service users know at first hand how well community care provision operates in some respects and how badly in others. Both groups need to exert a strong voice in determining the way forward.

Bibliography

Age Concern (1986) *The Law and Vulnerable People* (London: Age Concern).

Adams, R., Dominelli, L. and Payne, M. (1998) *Social Work: Themes, Issues and Critical Debates* (London: Macmillan).

Ahmad, W. I. U. (1996) 'Family Obligations and Social Change Among Asian Communities' in Ahmad, W. I. U. and Atkin, K. (eds) *Race and Community Care* (Buckingham: Open University Press).

Ahmad, W. I. U. and Atkin, K. (eds) (1996) *Race and Community Care* (Buckingham: Open University Press).

Aitken, L. and Griffin, G. (1996) *Gender Issues in Elder Abuse* (London: Sage).

Allen, I. and Perkins, E. (1995) *The Future of Family Care* (London: HMSO).

Ambache, J. (1997) 'Vulnerability and Public Responses', in Decalmer, P. and Glendenning, F. (1997) (2nd edn) *The Mistreatment of Elderly People* (London: Sage).

Arber, S. and Ginn, J. (1991) *Gender and Later Life: A Sociological Analysis of Resources and Constraints* (London: Sage).

Arber, S. and Ginn, J. (1995) 'Gender Differences in Informal Caring', *Health and Social Care in the Community*, 3 (1).

Atkin, K. and Rollings J. (1993) *Community Care in a Multi-Racial Britain: A Critical Review of the Literature* (London: HMSO).

Atkin, K. and Rollings, J. (1996) 'Looking After Their Own? Family Care-Giving Among Asian and Afro-Caribbean Communities', in Ahmad, W. I. U. and Atkin, K. (eds) *Race and Community Care* (Buckingham: Open University Press).

Attneave, C. (1969) 'Therapy in Tribal Settings and Urban Network Intervention', *Family Process*, 8, 182–210.

Audit Commission (1986) *Making a Reality of Community Care* (London: HMSO).

Audit Commission (1993) *Taking Care* (London: HMSO).

Audit Commission (1994) *Finding a Place: A Review of Mental Health Services For Adults* (London: HMSO).

Audit Commission (1996) *Balancing the Care Equation: Progress with Community Care* (Community Care Bulletin no. 3) (London: Audit Commission).

Audit Commission (1997) *The Coming of Age: Improving Care Services for Older People* (London: Audit Commission).

Audit Commission (1998) *Home Alone* (London: Audit Commission).

Audit Commission (1999) *First Assessment* (London: Audit Commission).

Baldock, J. and Ungerson, C. (1994) *Becoming Consumers of Community Care* (York: Joseph Rowntree Foundation).

Baldwin, S. (1997) 'Charging Users for Community Care', in May, M., Brunsdon, E. and Craig, G., *Social Policy Review 9* (London: Social Policy Association).

146

Barclay Report (1982) *Social Workers: Their Role and Tasks* (London: Bedford Square Press).

Barnes, J. A. (1954) 'Class and Committees in a Norwegian Island Parish', *Human Relations*, 7, 39–58.

Barnes, J. A. (1972) *Social Networks* (Reading, Mass.: Addison-Wesley).

Barnes, M. (1997) *Care, Communities and Citizens* (Harlow: Longman).

Barnes, M. and Warren, L. (1999) *Paths to Empowerment* (Bristol: The Policy Press).

Barr, A., Drysdale, J. and Henderson, P. (1997) *Towards Caring Communities* (Brighton: Pavilion).

Barry, M. and Hallett, C. (1998) *Social Exclusion and Social Work* (Lyme Regis: Russell House).

Bass, M. and Drewett, R. (1997) *Real Work: Supported Employment for People With Learning Difficulties* (Sheffield: Joint Unit for Social Services Research).

Baumhover, L. A. and Beall, S. C. (1996) *Abuse, Neglect and Exploitation of Older Persons* (London: Jessica Kingsley).

Bayley, M. (1973) *Mental Handicap and Community Care* (London: Routledge and Kegan Paul).

Becker, S. (1997) *Responding to Poverty* (London: Longman).

Bennett, G., Kingston, P. and Penhale, B. (1997) *The Dimensions of Elder Abuse* (London: Macmillan).

Beresford, P. (1997) 'The Last Social Division? Revisiting the Relationship Between Social Policy, its Producers and Consumers' in May, M., Brunsdon, E. and Craig, G. (eds), *Social Policy Review 9* (London: Social Policy Association).

Beresford, P. and Croft, S. (1993) *Citizen Involvement* (London: Macmillan).

Biegel, D. E., Shore, B. K. and Gordon, E. (1984) *Building Support Networks for the Elderly* (London: Sage).

Biggs, S. (1996) 'A Family Concern: Elder Abuse in British Social Policy', *Critical Social Policy*, 16 (2).

Biggs, S., Phillipson, C. and Kingston, P. (eds) (1995) *Elder Abuse in Perspective* (Buckingham: Open University Press).

Boissevain, J. and Mitchell, J. C. (1973) *Network Analysis: Studies in Human Interaction* (The Hague: Mouton).

Bott, E. (1957) *Family and Social Network* (London: Tavistock).

Bradley, G. and Manthorpe, J. (1997) *Dilemmas of Financial Assessment* (Birmingham: Venture).

Bradley, G., Manthorpe, J., Stanley, N. and Alaszewski, A. (1996) 'Training for Care Management: Using Research to Identify New Directions' *Issues in Social Work Education*, 16 (2), 27–45.

Brammer, A. (1996) 'Elder Abuse in the UK: A New Jurisdiction?' *Journal of Elder Abuse & Neglect*, 8 (2).

Brandon, D. (1995) *Advocacy* (Birmingham: Venture).

Braye, S. and Preston-Shoot, M. (1995) *Empowering Practice in Social Care* (Buckingham: Open University Press).

British Medical Association (1995) *Taking Care of the Carers* (London: BMA).

Brown, H. C. (1998) *Social Work and Sexuality* (London: Macmillan).

Brown, H. and Smith, H. (1992) *Normalisation* (London: Routledge).

Bulmer, M. (1987) *The Social Basis of Community Care* (London: Allen and Unwin).

Burns, D. and Taylor, M. (1998) *Mutual Aid and Self-Help* (Bristol: The Policy Press).

Butler, R. (1987) 'Agism' in *Encyclopaedia of Aging* (New York: Springer).

Campbell, J. and Oliver, M. (1996) *Disability Politics* (London: Routledge).

Campbell, P. (1966) 'The History of the User Movement in the United Kingdom' in Heller, T., Reynolds, J., Gomm, R., Muston, R. and Pattison, S. (eds), *Mental Health Matters* (Basingstoke: Macmillan).

Campbell, P. and Lindow, V. (1997) *Changing Practice: Mental Health Nursing and User Empowerment* (London: Mind and Royal College of Nursing).

Caplan, G. (1974a) 'Support Systems', in Caplan, G. (ed.), *Support Systems and Community Mental Health* (New York: Basic Books).

Caplan, G. (ed.) (1974b) *Support Systems and Community Mental Health* (New York: Basic Books).

Carers National Association (CNA) (1998) *The Carer* (London: CNA, March).

Cassel, J. (1974) 'Psychosocial Processes and Stress: Theoretical Formulations', *International Journal of Health Services*, 4, 471–82.

Challis, D. (1999) *Assessment and Care Management: Developments since the Community Care Reforms* in Royal Commission on Long Term Care, Research volume 3.

Challis, D. and Davies, B. (1986) *Case Management in Community Care* (London: Gower).

Challis, D., Darton, R., Johnson, L., Stone, M. and Traske, K. (1995) *Care Management and Health Care of Older People* (Aldershot: Arena).

CI (92) 34 (1992) Letter from Herbert Laming (chief social services inspector) on assessment, 14 December (London: DoH).

CI (95) 12 (1995) Chief inspector; letter on young carers (London: DoH).

Clapham, D. and Franklin, B. (1994) *Housing Management, Community Care and Competitive Tendering* (London: Chartered Institute of Housing).

Clarke, L. (1995) 'Family Care and Changing Family Structure: Bad News for the Elderly', in Allen, I. and Perkins, E. (eds), *The Future of Family Care* (London: HMSO).

Clarke, S. (1998) 'Community Development and Health Professionals', in Symonds, A. and Kelly, A. (eds), *The Social Construction of Community Care* (London: Macmillan).

Clements, L. (1996) *Community Care and the Law* (London: Legal Action Group).

Clifford, D. (1998) *Social Assessment Theory and Practice: A Multi-Disciplinary Framework* (Aldershot: Aldgate).

Clough, R. (1996) *The Abuse of Adults in Residential Institutions* (London: Whiting and Birch).

Cobb, S. (1976) 'Social Support as a Moderator of Life Stress', *Psychosomatic Medicine*, 38, 300–314.

Cohen, S. and Syme, S. L. (1985) *Social Support and Health* (London: Academic Press).

Collins, A. H. and Pancoast, D. L. (1976) *Natural Helping Networks* (Washington: National Association of Social Workers).

Cook-Daniels, L. (1997) 'Lesbian, Gay Male, Bisexual and Transgendered Elders: Elder Abuse and Neglect Issues', *Journal of Elder Abuse & Neglect*, 9 (2) (New York: The Hawarth Maltreatment and Trauma Press).

Cooper, H., Arber, S., Fee, L. and Ginn, J. (1999) *The Influence of Social Support and Social Capital on Health* (London: HEA).

Cooper, R., Watson, L. and Allan, G. (1994) *Shared Living* (London: JUSSR).

Cormie, J. (1999) 'The Fife User Panels Project: Empowering Older People', in Barnes, M. and Warren, L., *Paths to Empowerment* (Bristol: The Policy Press).

Craft, A. (1996) 'Abuse of Younger and Older People: Similarities and Difference', in Clough, R., *The Abuse of Adults in Residential Institutions* (London: Whiting & Birch).

Crewe, N. M. and Zola, I. K. (1983) *Independent Living for Physically Disabled People* (London: Jossey-Bass).

Croft, S. and Beresford, P. (1999) 'Elder Abuse and Participation: A Crucial Coupling for Change' in Slater, P. and Eastman, M. (eds), *Elder Abuse* (London: Age Concern).

Dalley, G. (1996) *Ideologies of Caring*, 2nd edn (London: Macmillan).

Dalley, G. (1989) 'Professional Ideology or Organisational Tribalism?', in Taylor, R. and Ford, J., *Social Work and Health Care* (London: Jessica Kingsley).

Dalrymple, J. and Burke, B. (1995) *Anti-Oppressive Practice: Social Care and the Law* (Buckingham: Open University Press).

Darvil, G. and Smale, G. (1990) *Partners in Empowerment: Networks of Innovation in Social Work* (London: National Institute of Social Work).

Davey, B. (1999) 'Solving Economic, Social and Environmental Problems Together: An Empowerment Strategy for Losers', in Barnes, M. and Warren, L. (eds), *Paths To Empowerment* (Bristol: The Policy Press).

Davies, B. P. and Challis, D. J. (1986) *Matching Resources to Needs in Community Care* (Aldershot: Gower).

Davis, A., Ellis, K. and Rummery, K. (1997) *Access to Assessment* (Bristol: The Policy Press).

Decalmer, P. and Glendenning, F. (eds) (1997) *The Mistreatment of Elderly People*, 2nd edn (London: Sage).

DHSS (1981) *Growing Older* (London: HMSO).

DHSS (Northern Ireland) (1990) *People First: Community Care in Northern Ireland* (Belfast: HMSO).

Dimond, B. (1997) *Legal Aspects of Care in the Community* (London: Macmillan).

Dobash, R. E. and Dobash, R. (1992) *Women, Violence and Social Change* (London: Routledge).

DoH (1989a) *Caring for People* (London: HMSO).

DoH (1989b) *Working for Patients* (London: HMSO).

DoH (1990) *Community Care in the Next Decade and Beyond: Policy Guidance* (London: HMSO).

DoH (1991a) *Care Management and Assessment: Managers' Guide* (London: HMSO).

DoH (1991b) *Care Management and Assessment: Practitioners' Guide* (London: HMSO).

DoH (1993) *No Longer Afraid: Practice Guidelines* (London: HMSO).

DoH (1994) *Key Area Handbook: Mental Illness*, 2nd edn (London: HMSO).

DoH (1995a) *Building Bridges* (London: DoH).

DoH (1995b) *Practical Guidance on Joint Commissioning for Project Leaders* (London: DoH).

DoH (1995c) *Child Protection: Messages from Research* (London: HMSO).

DoH (1996) *The Spectrum of Care: Local Services for People with Mental Health Problems* (London: HMSO).

DoH (1997a) *The New NHS – Modern, Dependable* (London: HMSO).

DoH (1997b) *Developing Partnerships in Mental Health* (London: DoH).

DoH (1997c) *Community Care (Direct Payments) Act (1996: Policy and Practice Guidance* (London: DoH).

DoH (1998a) *Modernising Social Services* (London: DoH).

DoH (1998b) *They Look After Their Own, Don't They?* (London: DoH).

DoH (1998c) *Modernising Mental Health Services* (London: DoH).

DoH (1998d) *Partnership in Action* (London: DoH).

DoH (1999a) *Caring About Carers* (London: DoH).

DoH (1999b) *Saving Lives: Our Healthier Nation* (London: DoH).

Douglas, A. and Philpot, T. (1998) *Caring and Coping* (London: Routledge).

DSS (1999) *Supporting People* (London: DSS).

Eastman, M. (1984) *Old Age Abuse* (Mitcham: Age Concern).

Eastman, M. (1994) *Old Age Abuse* (London: Chapman and Hall/Age Concern).

Eastman, M. (1999) 'Elder Abuse and Professional Intervention: A Social Welfare Model?', in Slater, P. and Eastman, M., *Elder Abuse* (London: Age Concern).

Ell, K. (1996) 'Social Networks, Social Support and Coping with Serious Illness: The Family Connection' in *Social Science and Medicine*, 42 (2), 173–83.

Ellis, K. (1993) *Squaring the Circle* (York: Joseph Rowntree Foundation).

Family Policy Studies Centre (1997) *A Guide to Family Issues: Family Briefing Paper 2* (London: Family Policy Studies Centre).

Finch, J. (1989) *Family Obligations and Social Change* (Cambridge: Polity Press).

Finch J. (1995) 'Responsibilities, Obligations and Commitments', in Allen, I. and Perkins, E., *The Future of Family Care* (London: HMSO).

Finch, J. and Groves, D. (eds) (1983) *A Labour of Love: Women, Work and Caring* (London: RKP).

Finch, J. and Mason, J. (1993) *Negotiating Family Responsibilities* (London: Routledge).

Fischer, C. (1982) *To Dwell among Friends* (Chicago, Ill.: University of Chicago Press).

Freire, P. (1972) *Pedagogy of the Oppressed* (London: Penguin).

Friedman, S. R. (1999) *Social Networks, Drug Injectors' Lives and HIV/AIDs* (London: Plenum).

Froland, C., Pancoast, D. L., Chapman, N. J. and Kimboko, P. J. (1981) *Helping Networks and Human Services* (California: Sage).

Galanter (1999) *Network Therapy for Alcohol and Drug Abuse* (New York: Guilford Press).

Galvin, S. W. and McCarthy, S. (1994) 'Multi-Disciplinary Community Team: Clinging to the Wreckage', *Journal of Mental Health*, 3, 157–66.

Godfrey, J. (1999) 'Empowerment Through Sexuality' in Wilkinson, G. and Miers, M. (eds), *Power and Nursing Practice* (Basingstoke: Macmillan).

Gottlieb, B. H. (1983) *Social Support Strategies* (California: Sage).

Grant, L. (1999) *Remind Me Who I Am, Again* (London: Granta).

Green, H. (1988) *Informal Carers* (London: HMSO).

Griffiths, R. (1988) *Community Care: Agenda for Action* (London: HMSO).

Grundy, E. (1995) 'Demographic Influences on the Future of Family Care' in Allen, I. and Perkins, E. (eds), *The Future of Family Care* (London: HMSO).

Hadley, R. and Clough, R. (1996) *Care in Chaos* (London: Cassell).

Hancock, M. and Villeneau, R. (1997) *Effective Partnerships* (London: Sainsbury Centre).

Harding, T., Meredith, B. and Wistow, G. (1996) *Options for Long-Term Care* (London: HMSO).

HC(89)5 *Discharge of Patients from Hospital* (London: DoH).

Health Education Authority (HEA) (1998) *Putting Health on the Regeneration Agenda* (London: HEA).

Health Service Commissioner (1994) *Failure to Provide Long-Term NHS Care for a Brain-Damaged Patient*, HC(197 (London: HMSO).

Hennessy, D. (ed.) (1997) *Community Health Care Development* (London: Macmillan).

Henwood, M. (1998) *Ignored and Invisible? Carers' Experience of the NHS* (London: Carers National Association).

Heron, C. (1998) *Working with Carers* (London: Jessica Kingsley).

Hillery, G. A. (1955) 'Definitions of Community: Areas of Agreement', *Rural Sociology*, 50, 20–35).

Hoggett, P., Stewart, M., Razzaque, K. and Barker, I. (1999) *Urban Regeneration and Mental Health in London* (London: King's Fund).

Holman B. (1993) *A New Deal for Social Welfare* (Oxford: Lion Publishing).

Home Office (1998) *Speaking up for Justice* (London: Home Office).

House of Commons Health Committee (HOC) (1995) *Long-Term Care: NHS Responsibilities for Meeting Continuing Health Care Needs*, first report, vol 1–3 (London: HMSO).

House of Commons Health Committee (HOC) (1999) *The Relationship between Health and Social Services*, vol. 1 (London: Stationery Office).

Jack, R. (1995) *Empowerment in Community Care* (London: Chapman and Hall).

Kiernan, K. and Wicks, M. (1990) *Family Change and Future Policy* (London: Family Policy Studies Centre).

King's Fund Centre (1991) *Meeting the Challenge* (London: King Edward's Hospital Fund).

Kingston, P. and Penhale, B. (eds) (1995) *Family Violence and the Caring Professions* (London: Macmillan).

LAC(92)27 (1992) *National Assistance Act (1948 (Choice of Accommodation) Directions* (London: DoH).

LAC(93)4 (1993) *Community Care Plans (Consultation) Directions* (London: DoH).

LAC(95)5 (1995) *NHS Responsibilities for Meeting Continuing Health Care Needs* (London: DoH).

LAC(97)15 (1997) *Family Law Act (1996 Part 1V, Family Homes and Domestic Violence, Responsibilities of Local Authorities and the Guardian Ad Litem and Reporting Officer Service* (London: DoH).

Law Commission (1995 Mental Incapacity (London: HMSO).

Lawson, J. (1999) 'Developing a Policy on Abuse in Residential and Nursing Homes' in Pritchard, J. (ed.), *Elder Abuse Work* (London: Jessica Kingsley).

Leathard, A. (1994) *Going Inter-Professional* (London: Routledge).

Leathard, A. (1997) 'The New Boundaries of Health and Welfare in Collaborative Care', in May, M., Brunsdon, E. and Craig, G., *Social Policy Review 9* (London: Social Policy Association).

Lewis, J. and Glennerster, H. (1996) *Implementing the New Community Care* (Buckingham: Open University Press.

Lewis, J. and Meredith, B. (1988) *Daughters Who Care: Daughters Caring for Mothers at Home* (London: RKP).

Lipsky, M. (1980) *Street Level Bureaucracy: Dilemmas of the Individual in Public Services* (New York: Russell Sage Foundation).

Litwin, H. (1995) *Uprooted in Old Age* (Westport: Greenwood Press).

Litwin, H. (1997) 'Social Network Type and Health Service Utilization', *Research on Aging*, 19 (3), 274–99.

Litwin, H. (1998) 'Social Network Type and Health Status in a National Sample of Elderly Israelis', *Social Science and Medicine*, 46 (4–5), 599–609.

Litwin, H. (1999) 'Support Network Type and Patterns of Help Giving and Receiving Among Older Adults', *Journal of Social Service Research*, 24 (3/4), 83–101.

Local Government Association (LGA) (1997) *Removing the Barriers: The Case for a New Deal for Social Services and Social Security* (London: LGA).

Lord Chancellor's Department (1997) *Who Decides?* (London: HMSO).

Loxley, A. (1997) *Collaboration in Health and Welfare* (London: Jessica Kingsley).

Mandelstam, M. (1999) *Community Care Practice and the Law*, 2nd edn (London: Jessica Kingsley).

Manthorpe, J. (1999) 'Putting Elder Abuse on the Agenda: Achievements of a Campaign', in Slater, P. and Eastman, M., *Elder Abuse* (London: Age Concern).

Mares, P. (1996) *Business Skills for Care Management* (London: Age Concern).

May, M., Brunsdon, E. and Craig, G. (1997) *Social Policy Review 9* (London: Social Policy Association).

Mayer, P. (1961) *Tribesmen or Townsmen* (Cape Town: Oxford University Press).

Mayo, M. (1998) 'Community Work' in Adams, R., Dominelli, L. and Payne, M. (eds) (1998) *Social Work: Themes, Issues and Critical Debates* (London: Macmillan).

McCreadie, C. (1994) 'Introduction: The Issues, Practice and Policy', in Eastman, M., *Old Age Abuse* (London: Chapman and Hall).

McCreadie, C. (1996) *Elder Abuse: Update on Research* (London: Institute of Gerontology).

Means, R. and Smith, R. (1998) *Community Care: Policy and Practice*, 2nd edn (London: Macmillan).

Mencap (1999) *Fully Charged* (London: Mencap).

Mills, C. W. (1959) *The Sociological Imagination* (Oxford: Oxford University Press).

Mitchell, J. C. (1969) *Social Networks in Urban Situations* (Manchester: Manchester University Press).

Morris, J. (1991) *Pride against Prejudice* (London: The Women's Press).

Morris, J. (1993) *Independent Lives* (London: Macmillan).

Morris, J. (1997) *Community Care: Working in Partnership with Service Users* (Birmingham: Venture Press).

Mullender, A. (1996) *Rethinking Domestic Violence* (London: Routledge).

Nahmiash, D. (1999) 'From Powerlessness to Empowerment', in Pritchard, J. (ed.), *Elder Abuse Work* (London: Jessica Kingsley).

NCVO (1996) *Meeting the Challenge of Change* (London: NCVO).

Nocon, A. and Baldwin, S. (1998) *Trends in Rehabilitation Policy* (London: King's Fund).

Nolan, M., Grant, G. and Keady, J. (1996) *Understanding Family Care* (Buckingham: Open University Press).

North, C., Ritchie, J. and Ward, K. (1993) *Factors Influencing the Implementation of the Care Programme Approach* (London: HMSO).

Ogg, J. and Bennett, G. (1992) 'Elder Abuse in Britain', *British Medical Journal*, 305, 998–9.

Oliver, M. (1990) *The Politics of Disablement* (London: Macmillan).

Oliver, M. (1996) *Understanding Disability: From Theory to Practice* (Basingstoke: Macmillan).

Oliver, M. and Sapey, B. (1999) *Social Work with Disabled People* (Basingstoke: Macmillan).

Onyett, S. (1997) 'Collaboration and the Community Health Team', *Journal of Interprofessional Care*, 11 (3).

Onyett, S. and Ford, R. (1996) 'Multidisciplinary Community Teams: Where is the Wreckage', *Journal of Mental Health*, 5 (1), 47–55.

Onyett, S., Heppleston, T. and Bushnell, D. (1994) 'A National Survey of Community Mental Health Teams', *Journal of Mental Health*, 3, 175–94.

Onyett, S., Pillinger, T. and Muijen, M. (1995) *Making Community Mental Health Teams Work* (London: Sainsbury Centre for Mental Health).

Parker, G. and Lawton, D. (1994) *Different Types of Care, Different Types of Carer: Evidence from the General Household Survey* (London: HMSO).

Parkinson, M. (1998) *Combating Social Exclusion* (Bristol: Policy Press).

Patmore, C. and Weaver, T. (1991) *Community Mental Health Teams: Lessons for Planners and Managers* (London: Good Practices in Mental Health).

Payne, M. (1995) Social Work and Community Care (London: Macmillan).

Penhale, B. and Kingston, P. (1995) 'Social Perspectives on Elder Abuse', in Kingston, P. and Penhale, B. (eds), *Family Violence and the Caring Professions* (London: Macmillan).

Petch, A., Cheetham, J., Fuller, R., MacDonald, C. and Myers, F. (1996) *Delivering Community Care* (Edinburgh: The Stationery Office).

Pillemer, K. A. (1984) 'Social Isolation and Elder Abuse' *Response*, 8 (4), 2–4.

Pillemer, K. A. and Wolf, R. (eds) (1986) *Elder Abuse: Conflict in the Family* (New York: Auburn House).

Poxton, R. (1996) 'Bridging the Gap: Joint Commissioning of Health and Social Care', in Harrison, A., *Health Care UK 1995–1996* (London: King's Fund).

Priestley, M. (1999) *Disability Politics and Community Care* (London: Jessica Kingsley).

Pritchard, J. (1995) *The Abuse of Older People*, 2nd edn (London: Jessica Kingsley).

Pritchard, J. (1996) *Working with Elder Abuse: A Training Manual for Home Care,* Residential and Day Care Staff (London: Jessica Kingsley).

Pritchard, J. (ed.) (1999) *Elder Abuse Work* (London: Jessica Kingsley).

Qureshi, H. and Walker, A. (1989) *The Caring Relationship* (London: Macmillan).

Renshaw, J. (1988) 'Care in the Community: Individual Care Planning and Case Management', *British Journal of Social Work*, supplement, 18.

Richards, E. (1996) *Paying for Long-Term Care* (London: IPPR).

Ritchie, J., Dick, D. and Lingham, R. (1994) *The Report of the Inquiry into the Care and Treatment of Christopher Clunis* (London: HMSO).

Robb, B. (1967) *Sans Everything: A Case to Answer* (London: Thomas Nelson).

Robson, P., Locke, M. and Dawson, J. (1997) *Consumerism or Democracy* (Bristol: Policy Press).

Rowntree Foundation (1996) *Meeting the Costs of Continuing Care* (York: Joseph Rowntree Foundation).

Royal Commission on Long Term Care (RCLTC) (1999) *With Respect to Old Age* (London: Stationery Office) (main report and 3 volumes of evidence).

Rueveni, U. (1979) *Networking Families in Crisis* (New York: Human Sciences Press).

Sanders, A., Creaton, J., Bird, S. and Weber, L. (1997) *Victims with Learning Disabilities* (Oxford: Centre for Criminological Research, University of Oxford).

Scott, H. (ed.) (1999) *Speaking Out – On Elder Abuse within Ethnic Minority Communities*, working paper no. 3 (London: Action on Elder Abuse).

Seebohm Report (1968) *Report of the Committee on Local Authority and Allied Personal Services* (London: HMSO).

Sharkey, P. J. (1989) 'Social Networks and Social Service Workers', *British Journal of Social Work*, 19, 387–405.

Sharkey, P. J. (1995) *Introducing Community Care* (London: Collins Educational).

Sheppard, M. (1995) *Care Management and the New Social Work* (London: Whiting and Birch).

Simons, K. (1997) *A Foot in the Door* (Manchester: NDT).

Skellington, R. (1992) *Race in Britain Today* (London: Sage).

Slater, P. (1999) 'Elder Abuse as Harm to Older Adults: The Relevance of Age', in Slater, P. and Eastman, M., (eds) *Elder Abuse* (London: Age Concern).

Slater, P. and Eastman, M. (1999) (eds) *Elder Abuse* (London: Age Concern).

Smale, G., Tuson, G., Biehal, N. and Marsh, P. (1993) *Empowerment, Assessment, Care Management and the Skilled Worker* (London: HMSO).

Social Exclusion Unit (SEU) (1998) *Bringing Britain Together: A National Strategy for Neighbourhood Renewal* (London: HMSO).

Social Services Inspectorate (1998) *They Look After Their Own, Don't They?* (London: DoH).

Speck, R. and Attneave, C. (1973) *Family Networks* (New York: Pantheon).

Spokes, J., Pare, M. and Royle G. (1988) *The Report of the Committee of Inquiry into the Care and Aftercare of Miss Sharon Campbell* (London: HMSO).

Stalker, K., Baron, S., Riddell, S. and Wilkinson, H. (1999) 'Models of Disability: The Relationship Between Theory and Practice in Non-Statutory Organisations', *Critical Social Policy*, 19 (1).

Stevenson, O. (1996) *Elder Protection in the Community* (London: DoH).

Stewart, M. J. (1993) *Integrating Social Support and Nursing* (London: Sage).

Stockford, D. (1988) *Integrating Care Systems* (London: Longman).

Szivos, S. (1992) 'The Limits to Integration', in Brown, H. and Smith, H. (eds), *Normalisation* (London: Routledge).

Taylor, S. (1993) 'Social Integration, Social Support and Health', in Taylor, S. and Field, D. (eds), *Sociology of Health and Health Care* (Oxford: Blackwell).

Taylor. S. and Field, D. (1993) *Sociology of Health and Health Care* (Oxford: Blackwell).

Thomas, D. (1999) 'Disempowerment, Empowerment and Older People', in Wilkinson, G. and Miers, M. (eds), *Power and Nursing Practice* (London: Macmillan).

Thompson, N. (1995) *Age and Dignity* (Aldershot: Arena).

Thompson, N. (1997) *Anti-Discriminatory Practice*, 2nd edn (London: Macmillan).

Thompson, N. (1998) *Promoting Equality* (London: Macmillan).

Thornton, P. and Tozer, R. (1995) *Having a Say in Change: Older People and Community Care* (York: Joseph Rowntree Foundation).

Titmus, R. (1973) *The Gift Relationship* (London: Penguin).

Todhunter, C. (1998) *Exploring the Boundaries between Continuing Health and Social Care for Older People in Two Local Authorities*, unpublished MPhil thesis, Liverpool John Moores University.

Townsend, P. (1962) *The Last Refuge* (London: Routledge and Kegan Paul).

Trevillion, S. (1999) *Networking and Community Partnership* (Aldershot: Ashgate).

Trimble, D. and Kliman, J. (1995) in Elkaim, M. (ed.), *Panorama des Therapies Familiales* (Paris: Editions du Seuil).

Truax, C. B. and Carkhuff, R. R. (1967) *Towards Effective Counselling and Psychotherapy: Training and Practice* (New York: Aldine).

Turnbull, A. (1998) *Home from Home* (London: King's Fund).

Twigg, J. (1989) 'Models of Care: How do Social Care Agencies Conceptualise their Relationship with Informal Carers', *Journal of Social Policy*, 18 (1).

Twigg, J. (1992) *Carers; Research and Practice* (London: HMSO).

Twigg, J. and Atkin, K. (1994) *Carers Perceived* (Buckingham: Open University Press).

Ungerson, C. (1987) *Policy is Personal: Sex, Gender and Informal Caring* (London: Tavistock).

Utting, W. (1994) *Creating Community Care* (London: Mental Health Foundation).

Ward, L. (ed.) (1999) *Innovations in Advocacy and Empowerment for People with Intellectual Disabilities* (Chorley: Lisieux Hall Publications).

Wardhaugh, J. and Wilding, P. (1993) 'Towards an Explanation of the Corruption of Care', *Critical Social Policy*, 47, 4–31.

Wells, J. S. G. (1997) 'Priorities, "Street Level Bureaucracy" and the Community Mental Health Team', *Health and Social Care in the Community*, 5 (5), 333–42.

Wenger, G. C. (1984) *The Supportive Network: Coping with Old Age* (London: Allen & Unwin).

Wenger, G. C. (1994) *Support Networks of Older People: A Guide for Practitioners* (Bangor: Centre For Social Policy Research and Development, University of Wales).

Wenger, G. C. and Day, B. (1995) *Support Networks of Older People* (Brighton: Pavilion Publishing).

Whittaker, T. (1995) 'Violence, Gender and Elder Abuse: Towards a Feminist Analysis and Practice', *Journal of Gender Studies*, 4 (1), 35–45.

Whittaker, J. K. and Garbarino, J. (1993) *Social Support Networks* (New York: Aldine).

Wilkinson, G. and Miers, M. (1999) *Power and Nursing Practice* (London: Macmillan).

Williams, P. and Shoultz, B. (1982) *We Can Speak for Ourselves* (London: Souvenir).

Wistow, G. and Brooks, T. (1988) *Planning and Joint Management* (London: RIPA).

Wistow, G (1995) 'Paying for Long-Term Care: The Shifting Boundary between Health and Social Care', *Community Care Management and Plannning*, 3 (3), 81–9.

Wistow, G., Knapp, M., Hardy, B., Forder, J., Kendall, J. and Manning, R. (1996) *Social Care Markets* (Buckingham: Open University Press).

Wistow, G. (1997) 'Funding Long Term Care', in May, M., Brunsdon, E. and Craig, G. (eds), *Social Policy Review 9* (London: Social Policy Association).

Wolfenden Report (1978) *The Future of Voluntary Organisations: Report of the Wolfenden Committee* (London: Croom Helm).

Wolfensberger, W. (1972) *The Principle of Normalisation in Human Services* (Toronto: National Institute on Mental Retardation).

Index

Note: entries in **bold** denote some form of illustrative material.